HAVING A BABY Can Be A Scream

by Joan Rivers

Introduction by Morrison S. Levbarg, M.D.

Illustrated by Frank Page

Published by J. P. Tarcher, Inc., Los Angeles

Distributed by Hawthorn Books, New York

To Melissa
Without whom I wouldn't have needed this book
and
To Edgar
Without whom I wouldn't have had Melissa

Contents

LETTER FROM A REAL DOCTOR—

Joan Rivers is aptly named, for, like a river, she goes on and on...

Seriously, Joan - again like a river - has sparkle, vitality and depth. All these qualities are apparent in her book on a subject as old and broad as the Mississippi itself - Motherhood and Childcare.

Make no mistake. In between the inevitable gag lines, there are plenty of useful hints and sensible solutions to problems every young parent faces. Because Joan has almost total recall, she can trace her own experiences throughout prgnancy and her child's early years. Laugh along with her, but you will learn while you are laughing!

This book makes parenthood fun. It takes some of the fear and uncertainty out of situations that are brand-new and happening so quickly in the lives of its readers. Happily, its humorous viewpoint never interferes with its serious intent to help many young parents to relax and enjoy their children.

So, my advice to you is: Get out your goldrush pan and go prospecting. You'll find many golden nuggets of information in one of the fastest moving Rivers of them all -

Morrisn S. Levbarg MD

When my husband, Edgar, and I were courting, he said he couldn't wait to have a baby. It was only after we were married that he changed his mind and decided that I should have the baby. And that's when I got frightened.

Like most women, I had always wanted children, but when my rabbit finally died I was fraught with questions. Was I ready to become a mother? Did I know enough? Would the baby and I survive my amateur bumblings? And did the rabbit leave a will? Well, I was, I did, we have, and he didn't.

And that's why I am writing this book. To let every pregnant woman (and man) out there know that you can smile your way in and out of the maternity ward. And all through motherhood, too. Well, almost.

Having a baby and becoming a mother should be a ball. Not a bawl. And yet throughout history women have passed down such tales of horror to each other ("I was in labor 108 days." "My doctor left more stitches in me than in an entire knit dress." "They had to give me gas, plus a spinal, plus ether—and I still felt everything!") that almost every pregnant woman approaches the big event with fear and trepidation. As a matter of fact, some of the bravest decided not to have children at all, including: Joan of Arc, Florence Nightingale, and Gloria Steinem, who, rumor has it, insisted on having a vasectomy.

Six years ago I was almost one of them. I was scared silly. Mainly because my cousin Shirley, who never complains, screamed and screamed when she was having her baby. True, this was just during *conception.* But it put me off.

So I started asking around exactly what was what. I called and interviewed dozens of obstetricians, pediatricians and one chiropodist by mistake. I started asking them questions, questions, questions. Each one kindly gave me answers, answers, answers. (Except one obstetrician, who in order to avoid me moved to China and is now delivering babies by acupuncture.)

Mainly because of these conversations, and the knowledge that I acquired from them, when my Big Day came (January 20, 1968), it was joyous and exciting—and well worth the minor pain and discomfort I suffered when I broke two front teeth while biting down on a bullet.

Having a Baby Can Be a Scream is a summary of the dialogues that I had with many experts (who didn't always agree with each other) —and the chiropodist—but mostly it is the distillation of my exchanges with Dr. Morrison Levbarg, a most distinguished Park Avenue pediatrician whose offices—and billing system—were always open and waiting for me.

And so, mama-to-be, sit down, prop this book on your tummy and read. This isn't meant to replace Dr. Spock. So keep him beside you. (But don't tell Mrs. Spock.) I hope these dialogues will also be a good bed companion in the absence of the real thing. So keep smiling. Remember, you never looked more radiant . . . from the neck UP.

JOAN RIVERS

CHAPTER I

Doctor, Why Are You Carrying That Dead Rabbit?

I'll never forget the first signs I had that made me think maybe I was pregnant. I found myself throwing up every morning, even when I wasn't thinking about Edgar's family, and I began to wake up in the middle of the night craving food instead of my husband. Finally I began to notice that I was having a harder and harder time seeing my toes, so I toddled off to my doctor. "Doc," I said to him, "how do I know I'm pregnant?" He told me the first sign of pregnancy was a missed period. That didn't sound too bad. What he didn't tell me was that a baby nine months later was the second.

Of course, there are many other signs in between—such as enlargement and increasing sensitivity of the breasts and dizziness and nausea—but if you want to know fast, as I did, you can take a rabbit test as early as two weeks after you have missed your first period.

A word of caution should go in here. Rabbit tests are only 90% accurate. There can be slip-ups. Two tragedies, for example, come to mind. The first is my friend Harriet. Harriet took the rabbit test, but instead of dying, the rabbit turned gay. (Interestingly enough too, Harriet's baby turned out to be a hairdresser.)

Another friend of mine, Jane, got a sick rabbit and at the very moment of the test it dropped dead of a stroke. Poor Jane naturally thought she was pregnant, but nine months later the only thing that was delivered to her was the decorator's bill for turning her den into a baby's room.

Anyhow, whether you take a rabbit test or not, take advantage of the fact that you live in America and go to an obstetrician. I remember asking my doctor . . .

Joan: How does one go about finding the best obstetrician? Go to the golf club on Wednesdays?

Doctor: Your women friends who are already mothers will clamor to solve this problem for you. Each woman always thinks *her* obstetrician is the best. As with any kind of doctor, his first qualification must be that he inspires confidence in you. Remember, your relationship with your obstetrician will help make this a safe and easy journey.

Joan: What is this safe and easy journey going to cost me?

Doctor: There is no set fee. Each obstetrician more or less has an average fee for his community, which most of his patients will pay. The best approach is an open one.

Joan: With a pocketbook to match.

Doctor: Come, come, Miss Rivers, surely you're not . . .

Joan: Broke? My husband keeps saying we are. But that's impossible. I still have checks left. Anyhow, we have hospitalization. That should help, don't you think?

Doctor: Have a candid discussion with your doctor at the very beginning about his fees. Remember, your doctor is a D*O*C*T*O*R and deserves a little respect. What does this white jacket tell you?

Joan: That you moonlight as a Good Humor man?

Doctor: Very few doctors today are wealthy. Why, just the high cost of living, keeping up a modern office—do you think Mies van der Rohe chairs come cheap?—not to mention bandages, aspirin and greens fees!

Joan: How often should I see my obstetrician?

Doctor: During the first half of your pregnancy, assuming all goes well, you should visit your doctor once a month. For the next several months, you might be asked to see him every two or three weeks. In the last month or so, weekly visits are the usual practice 'til the baby arrives.

Joan: I guess I should be home when the kid arrives. It makes a better impression.

Doctor: I would suggest a hospital.

Joan: Doc, I'm from a small town—Larchmont. The only hospital we have is Fred's Hospital & Grill and somehow I find it hard to trust a doctor whose sterilizer has hot dogs in it.

Doctor: You should check out the hospital of your choice carefully, especially to find out what their attitude is toward rooming in or natural childbirth. Again, your obstetrician can help here. He'll arrange for accommodations for you.

Joan: How will he know the date my baby's due?

Doctor: The doctors usually figure on 280 days from the first day of your last menstrual period. But no one knows exactly how long it will take your baby to develop. Be patient. Two weeks one way or the other should not be alarming.

11

Joan: Unless, of course, I'm in labor for those two weeks.

Doctor: You look like a nice, normal, healthy girl. I hardly think that will happen—not with proper care and exercise.

Joan: Exercise?!! Doctor, I'm Jewish. Jews don't exercise. We sell the equipment.

Doctor: Well, actually, strenuous exercises such as tennis, golf and riding are not especially recommended. Swimming is permissible if you avoid diving, violent surf and extremely cold water.

Joan: What would you recommend for me?

Doctor: Most doctors advise a healthy woman to walk every day even though she's doing housework. The important point is to stop before you're tired.

Joan: Oh, I never get tired of housework.

Doctor: Really?

Joan: I don't do any. When guests come to visit, I just put out drop cloths and say we're painting.

Doctor: Today we feel it is advisable for a woman to go on working while pregnant if she is in good health and if she wants to continue working. Most women maintain a healthier point of view during pregnancy if their way of life is not changed too sharply.

Joan: How long can a woman keep working?

Doctor: In fairly sedentary work, there's no reason why she can't continue on the job into her ninth month.

Joan: A friend of mine worked up until the end. She even had her baby right at work!

Doctor: What does she do?

Joan: She's a Delivery Room nurse.

Doctor: If she did work during her pregnancy, I hope she had a helping hand at home with the more strenuous housekeeping duties.

Joan: Oh, yes, her mother-in-law. She was always right there to help her throw out the empties.

Doctor: Anything more than light drinking during pregnancy is bad, and smoking ideally should be "out" for everybody pregnant. If you're a heavy smoker and can't quit, at least you should cut down. Moderate intakes of alcohol have no serious effect on either the mother or her unborn child. But drinking to the point of intoxication is bad on many counts. Being drunk makes a person more prone to accidental injury and drinks are high in "empty calories," to name two.

Joan: And speaking of two, how about sex?

Doctor: Miss Rivers, I'm a married man!

Joan: Oh, not with you! I meant with Edgar—or someone who looks a lot like him—like Paul Newman.

Doctor: For a while it may have to be with no one. Some doctors believe that the time when a woman would be having a period if she were not pregnant is an especially vulnerable one and that intercourse—as well as all other strenuous activities—should be eliminated then. Other doctors say a woman shouldn't have intercourse during the first three months. However, there are many conflicting opinions. I personally believe that sexual activity is permissible as long as it is comfortable and pleasurable.

Joan: So that's what it's supposed to be like! What about sex toward the end of pregnancy?

Doctor: Most obstetricians recommend no sexual relationships during the last six weeks, but as they say, "Love will find a way."

Joan: "They" say a lot of things, Doc, but it doesn't help. For example, Whenever I'm worried they say, "Relax, one day your ship will come in."

Doctor: What's wrong with that?

Joan: I'm scared my ship will be the Titanic!

CHAPTER II

Be Glad You're Pregnant

When I found out I was pregnant, I was thrilled. It made me feel just like a high school girl again. Also, my condition really proved most eloquently the fact that I was loved—if only for a moment. And best of all, it scotched those vicious lies about my age that the girls at the bridge club were spreading as it's impossible to be pregnant AND post-menopausal at the same time.

The only drawback was that as I got farther into my pregnancy, my clothes began to get tighter, and finally I had to put away my caftans and muu-muus and get some maternity clothes. The styles were charming, but who was I kidding? I knew that sooner or later, no matter what I put on, it would end up looking like a tent with a bow on top.

One terrific thing that happened was the way my breasts developed. It was probably the only time in my life that I could look into a mirror and ask, "Mirror, Mirror, on the wall, who is the fairest of them all?" and not have the mirror answer, "You are, Sir." However, I didn't know about undergarments, and I remember asking my doctor . . .

Joan: Should I wear a maternity girdle?

Doctor: Only if you're pregnant. And only if you've been wearing a girdle. A light two-way stretch maternity girdle is good, and don't worry about its being too tight. Your baby floats in water which cannot be compressed. If the girdle feels all right to you, then it can't be hurting the baby.

Joan: What about maternity brassieres? Do I need one? Remember, I'm a liberated woman. Well, half liberated. When my friends all burned their bras, I burned just one cup.

Doctor: You do need a brassiere during pregnancy. But there's no need for any special type of support brassiere. As your breasts develop, a larger brassiere will become necessary. Remember, you will be gaining twenty or more pounds. That's why you need the support. As for stockings, those blue ones you have on are a bit much.

Joan: I'm not wearing any stockings.

Doctor: Well, if I were you, I'd slip into some support stockings or elastic bandages to help you with those varicose veins. Also, it helps to lie down often during the day and use pillows to prop your legs up so they are higher than your hips.

Joan: What causes varicose veins?

Doctor: Poor circulation. Plus an inherited tendency to have them. Round garters and rolled stockings, which constrict the veins, can produce varicose veins in women who otherwise would not tend to have them.

Joan: I read that a woman shouldn't bathe during the last six weeks of pregnancy. Is that true?

Doctor: Absolutely.

Joan: Don't you get a little gamey toward the end?

Doctor: Just take showers instead of baths. Also keep away from douching and bidets during your entire pregnancy.

Joan: So that's what a bidet is for! I always just put my feet in and play boats.

Doctor: Another thing you should do is see your dentist. During pregnancy your chances of getting cavities are greater. You may use the usual types of anesthesia, providing you've had no adverse reactions previously. Also, properly covered, you can have X-rays taken.

Joan: Great! I wanted to give Edgar a picture of me for Christmas, and the way I look now the only thing I'd dare give him is an X-ray.

Doctor: Now, now. Most women are at their most beautiful when they're pregnant. People will say, "Look, she's glowing."

Joan: It's from the heartburn! Another thing, Doctor—people keep saying I'm eating for two. Who are these two people? And why can't they do their own eating?

Doctor: That's just an expression meaning you are eating for yourself and the baby. But don't take it to mean you are allowed to gorge yourself. You must watch your figure during pregnancy.

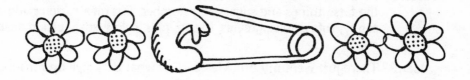

Joan: During pregnancy, I'll be the only one who *will* be watching my figure.

Doctor: You must not gain more than 20 pounds while you're pregnant, as too much weight may cause complications. Also, it's very hard to lose the weight afterward. But if a woman is careful about what she eats, she won't have this problem.

Joan: In other words, if it tastes good, spit it out.

Doctor: Eat a well-balanced diet with sufficient bulk from leafy vegetables to help with natural elimination. A good portion of meat, fish and eggs every day. Liver at least once a week. Grain products—preferably whole-grain breads and cereals. And, of course, a multivitamin

17

supplement with minerals and iron which the doctor will prescribe.

Joan: Ha! Doctor, I caught you. You forgot the most important thing: Milk! Every day she must drink milk!

Doctor: A woman doesn't have to drink milk if it's objectionable to her. She can consume it in other ways, such as in cream soups, custards, creamed vegetables. However, milk is rightfully called the most perfect food and contains the minerals needed for baby's bones and teeth, as well as being rich in so many other nutrients.

Joan: In general, I gather I should go heavy on the protein: meat, eggs, seafood, cheese, milk. A pregnant woman needs 50% more protein than she normally would. Correcto, Doc?

Doctor: Right. How come you're so smart?

Joan: 'Cause I'm writing this book. And the least I can do is keep one step ahead of you.

Doctor: So then you know about all the foods you shouldn't be eating. All the fatso things and sugars and starches. Fat meats, rich puddings, candy, soft drinks, gravies, bacon, pies, cakes, spaghetti, macaroni, etc.

Joan: There just went my breakfasts. Now what do I give up for lunch and dinner?

Doctor: Miss Rivers, if you were really thin I would tell you this is the perfect time to gain weight. There is no definite relationship between weight gained in pregnancy and the size of your child. So no need to worry that gaining too much weight will make the baby larger and delivery more difficult. The largest portion of the baby is the head, which has no fat deposits.

Joan: Then how come the world is so full of fatheads?

Doctor: Miss Rivers, that joke makes me ill!

Joan: Maybe it's morning sickness. I have a great cure for it: don't get up 'til afternoon.

Doctor: There are ways to avoid morning sickness. Try eating something before you get up.

Joan: How can you eat while you're asleep?

Doctor: I mean before you get out of bed. Something bland, dry and a bit filling. Like saltines or melba toast. Then stay in bed for another half hour. Also, to avoid nausea during the day, don't let your stomach feel empty. Keep things handy to nibble on, such as cheese, dried fruits and nuts.

Joan: How long does morning sickness go on? Into the middle of the night?

Doctor: It's usually over by the end of two and a half to three months.

Joan: What about medicines? Can I keep taking the pills I used to take?

Doctor: What pills did you take?

Joan: Birth control pills.

Doctor: No. Be particularly careful to use only those drugs your doctor approves for you. Then there's no chance that the developing embryo can be harmed.

Joan: Yes, but what about me? Will pregnancy leave me a marked woman for life?

Doctor: You mean the stretch marks that may appear during the last months of pregnancy? The answer is no. After the baby, they will gradually become smaller and thinner and eventually they will become only faint silvery streaks.

Joan: What can I do to prevent them?

Doctor: Nothing, really. Whether such streaks appear and how streaked your skin becomes depends in part on how much your stomach expands because of the size of your baby and how much excess fat you acquire. These marks can be minimized by avoiding any rapid gains. Many authorities recommend massaging your tummy with lanolin or cold cream daily during the last four months to ease the stretched condition of your skin.

Joan: Pregnancy is sure a fun time for a woman. I've heard that another tippy-top blessing a lot of us can look forward to is acne.

Doctor: The acne, when it occurs, is temporary and no special treatment is required, though some doctors recommend a particular soap. Anyway, I wouldn't worry about acne, unless you had it when you were an adolescent. Did you have a skin problem as a teenager?

Joan: Did I! I had such a skin condition that for two and a half years I was quarantined for chicken pox. Which is one of the reasons I can't wait to buy my "mask of pregnancy." Where do I get it and will I be able to use any of my credit cards?

Doctor: The mask of pregnancy refers to a brownish discoloration which may appear on the face during pregnancy, but which fades gradually after delivery, like a sunburn.

Joan: Who gets these masks?

Doctor: Mostly women who have had a history of poor nutrition.

Joan: What about freckles? Are they due also to poor nutrition?

Doctor: No. During pregnancy your skin takes up brown pigments more rapidly. Either from exposure to the sun or wherever there has been any inflammation or scar tissue formation.

Joan: Well, now, let me tick off all my glamorous features. I'll have silvery streaks, varicose veins, a mask and freckles. Oh, and I've heard my glorious halo of hair will become dry and break off.

HAVING A BABY   IS DEFINITELY   A LABOR   OF LOVE

Doctor: Don't worry about hair breaking off and getting dry. After the baby is born, it will return to normal. But meanwhile, brush your hair regularly and massage your scalp.

Joan: Doc, there must be some other really kicky, giggly things that could happen to me. Tell me, tell me, tell me. . . .

Doctor: Well, you could break out in rashes because of your tendency to perspire. So bathe and powder those surfaces that are likely to become moist.

Joan: Does that include my mouth?

Doctor: Also, headaches are likely to occur during the first three months of pregnancy. Especially among women who suffer pre-menstrual headaches. Just treat them as you would ordinary headaches.

Joan: I usually treat a headache by taking two aspirins.

Doctor: That's fine.

Joan: Which I rub on my forehead.

Doctor: Headaches aside, during the last weeks of pregnancy your sleep may be disturbed for a number of reasons. The strong activity of your baby and the pressure of the enlarged abdomen make it difficult for you to find a position which is comfortable for any length of time. Try hot milk. Or the classic ploy of counting sheep, or with your obstetrician's permission, you might take a sleeping pill.

Joan: When will the baby become a pain in the neck, or should I say, the stomach?

Doctor: During the last weeks. When the baby is growing large and heavy and the abdominal cavity feels crowded. But pain may also be felt over the bladder region—where the head of the baby is likely to press—or in the hip or the groin or along the margin of the lowest rib on either the right or the left side. But none of these pains is really significant. All of them can be alleviated with aspirin.

Joan: Come on, Doc. Sometimes I really wonder if the baby is worth all this. Pains—and more pains—and looking ugly are all you can promise me.

Doctor: Ah, but all your sufferings will be worthwhile once the patter of little feet is heard around the house.

Joan: I already hear the patter of little feet. I have a miniature dachshund.

Doctor: I'm sure your husband can cheer you up. Let him help you with household chores and let him take you out to dinner often.

Joan: Are you kidding? Yesterday I said, "Edgar, I'd like to eat out." He kicked my plate onto the fire escape.

Doctor: Miss Rivers, a husband should be involved with the pregnancy. Isn't your husband pleased you're pregnant?

Joan: I'm not so sure. When I telephoned to tell him the great news, he put me on "hold."

Doctor: Isn't he excited about the big event?

Joan: The only big event to him is the daily double.

Doctor: Well, you must involve your husband. For example, let him purchase the basic wardrobe which should consist of four shirts, diapers, four nightgowns, three kimonos and two receiving blankets.

Joan: Great, but what will the baby need?

Doctor: That's exactly what the baby will need. Along with a room of his own—if possible.

Joan: Why should the kid be lucky enough to have a room of his own when I still have to share mine with my husband?

Doctor: It will help him build better sleeping habits.

Joan: I've told my husband the same thing. That climbing onto the top bunk every night is getting to be a drag.

Doctor: The baby's room should be quiet, well ventilated and easily heated. It is important that the humidity be kept at a proper level so the baby's nose and mouth membranes won't dry out. Some people use a bassinet at first, but get a crib for the baby within six weeks to two months. Get one with a side that can be raised or lowered and with a firm mattress that can also be raised or lowered. The mattress should be at hip level during the first few months, so you don't have to stoop to lift the baby.

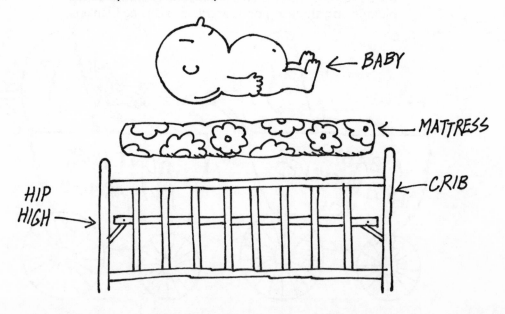

Joan: What else is needed?

Doctor: Two or three absorbent mattress pads and about four or six sheets. The fitted kind. And remember: the baby's sheets should be changed each time they are soiled and at the very least three times a week. Also, make sure you have four cotton blankets and two heavier ones. Cleanliness is a must for a baby.

Joan: Thank God, they soon grow out of it. What else should be in the baby's room?

Doctor: A wardrobe or chest to keep his clothes in. A comfortable chair for you and a steady table next to it to hold the feeding paraphernalia. Also, you'll need something with a hip level surface to change and dress the baby on. The top of a low chest of drawers will do—if it's well padded. Make sure there are straps to hold the baby down so he won't roll off.

Joan: I know just the kind of straps you mean. My husband attached those to our bed on our wedding night. Was *that* a disaster.

Doctor: Miss Rivers, *please,* I really don't want to know . . .

Joan: Some men smoke after making love—Edgar smoked during. And he had the nerve to ask me for a light. I said, "Get it yourself from the dashboard and don't disturb the bus driver."

SEYMOUR XAVIER SCHAINHOLZ, M.D.

Dearest Joanie,

I assume by the time you get this, you and little Melissa will be well ensconced and happy at home.

You were such a good patient and you gave me so many good laughs, I almost hate to bring up the delicate matter of remuneration. But to paraphrase an old saying, "Doctor, cannot live by laughs alone"--(unless those laughs will keep you in stitches. Ha, ha).

I am sure a celebrity of your stature is accustomed to being "comped" much of the time in restaurants and hotels and night clubs and the like and something you said here one day gave me the impression you had the impression your baby would also be "on the house."

However, as you know, a great deal of my practice is made up of celebrities and I ask you to consider where I'd be if I started "comping" my patients.

Anyhow, I'm sorry to have to bring the matter up at all and please be understanding about the embarrassing necessity of presenting you with a bill.

Your most humble and grateful physician,

[signature]

CHAPTER III

Just Because You're Lying Down, Doesn't Mean You're Lying In

No woman really likes to go to a hospital unless she's cozy with some doctor. But if one must do "time" at a hospital, it's nice to come back with a little bundle. Especially if that little bundle is filled with a baby.

To help prepare myself for the blessed event, I exercised all through pregnancy, even though it looked silly. Did you ever see a bunch of pregnant women running around a gym? We looked like a volleyball game where every player had the ball.

I also took a natural childbirth course. It was terrific. They used to put all of us pregnant mommies into gym suits and lay us down on the gym floor to do our exercises. We looked like a relief map of the Rocky Mountains. They explained everything that would happen during labor. At the end, they even showed a movie of a woman giving birth to her baby. I enjoyed that part the most. But for some reason, they threw me out of class. Maybe it was because I asked them to run the movie backward. "Come on, nurse," I shouted, "now let's see the baby disappear."

However, when the time came, I didn't have natural childbirth. I had a Jewish Delivery. They knocked me out when I had the first pain and woke me up when my hairdresser, Mr. Phyllis, got there.

And was I glad he came. I had no brush or comb with me. I had been so nervous when I was packing my bag. You see, I didn't listen when my doctor told me at the start of the ninth month, "It's good to pack your bag and have it ready—just in case."

The girls I grew up with all seemed to be packed up in their fifth month. I can remember the Larchmont paper was always carrying an item that started out, "Born prematurely to Mr. and Mrs. Dick Bizzy was a 14-pound baby boy."

Of course, I still have a bag I packed when I was single. I used to call it my Motel Survival Kit. . . .

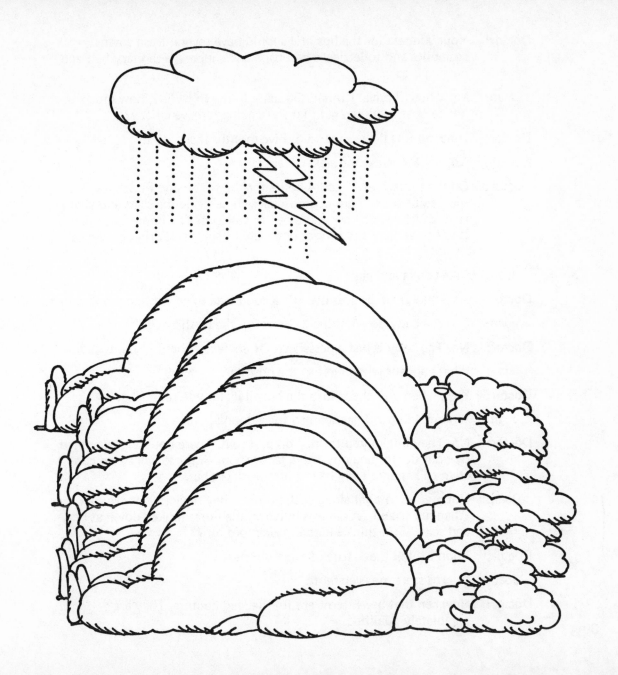

Doctor:	Your suitcase for the hospital should have several fresh gowns, cosmetics and toiletries, a bathrobe and slippers, a sanitary belt and nursing bras.
Joan:	My Motel Survival Kit had the same things in it! Say, how much notice does a woman get that she's going to have a baby?
Doctor:	Nine months if she's married. Five months if she isn't.
Joan:	No, no, I mean at the start of labor.
Doctor:	On the average of 12 to 24 hours for the first baby. Fewer for succeeding ones. Your obstetrician will describe the signs and symptoms of labor and how and when to call him. The important thing is not to eat any solid foods once labor begins and drink only clear liquids.
Joan:	Like vodka and gin?
Doctor:	As *un*like them as possible. It's a good idea to go off booze altogether.
Joan:	Can the baby do anything to hurry up the birth?
Doctor:	No. The baby is just a passenger. Or an "easy rider" if you will.
Joan:	What happens when I get to the hospital?
Doctor:	Well, when you check into the hospital and you're in labor—
Joan:	I know, I know. I get charged for a double.
Doctor:	No. They'll take you to the "prep" room. There you'll be examined by your doctor and put into a labor room. A nurse will be on constant call and you will have a buzzer to get her.
Joan:	Not me. I don't get along with nurses. They're vicious to women. When my friend Trudie was in labor, the nurse looked down at her and said, "Still think blondes have more fun?"
Doctor:	I don't think that's true of most nurses.
Joan:	Interns scare me even more.
Doctor:	How can that be? Interns are full-fledged doctors. They are completely qualified.

Joan: They're too young. How can you have confidence in a doctor who has his rubber gloves pinned to his sleeves? My sister had an intern so young, when he bent over to examine her, a box of Dots fell out of his pocket. She found it hard to have trust in him, especially when they got into the delivery room.

Doctor: Why?

Joan: He saw the bars on the windows and began to shout, "How will the stork get in?"

Doctor: I'll grant you delivery rooms aren't the homiest-looking places in the world. But you won't be there very long. Unless you're having natural childbirth, as soon as you get there, they'll put you on the delivery table and the doctor will give you an anesthetic.

Joan: Where will my husband be while I'm putting out in the delivery room?

Doctor: It doesn't matter as long as he's not underfoot. Once the baby is born, he is more than welcome. But never forget, in this performance it's the mother and the baby who are the stars.

Joan: Doctor, here is what I am trying to say. It's not that I don't trust my husband. (Ha-ha-ha.) But I had a friend, Muriel. While she was in labor, her husband Manny was getting tipsy with a nurse, and as a joke, they short-sheeted her bed.

Doctor: Miss Rivers, don't you trust your husband?

Joan: I used to. Then as a joke I got into a taxi and said to the driver, "Where can a girl get a little action in this town?" He took me to Edgar's office!

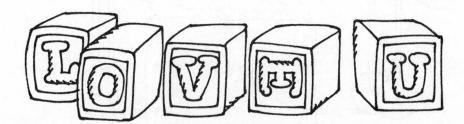

CHAPTER IV

Coming Home, Cutting Up and Putting Out

I will never forget the day I came home from the hospital. Even though I had only been gone a week, the apartment looked great— just the way I had left it—filthy. For all during pregnancy I hadn't bothered to clean. I felt that why should I bother to vacuum a rug that I couldn't see when I looked down?

The main reason I was glad to be home was that I'd been told I couldn't leave the hospital until I'd paid my bill, and knowing my insurance company, I figured by the time they settled my bill the kid would be a high school dropout.

Speaking of my kid, I must admit when I first saw her, she was no beauty. I had been told that most children were quite homely at birth, but I really wasn't prepared for what I got. Her eyes were closed, her legs were bowed and her hair was wet and matted. I couldn't believe it—she looked just like Edgar's side of the family. By the time we left the hospital, however, she was adorable, which is a good thing because if she hadn't been—as I told my doctor . . .

Joan: I would have switched kids.

Doctor: No way. They have all kinds of systems today to make certain the mothers go home with their own babies. Identification bracelets, footprints, thumbprints and so on. I guess you could say, "To each his own."

Joan: How long after the baby is born can I get up?

Doctor: The sooner the better. Usually within 24 hours after the great happening.

Joan: Just like on my honeymoon!

Doctor: The longer a person stays in bed, the weaker he feels on getting up. Walking is good for circulation. Today obstetricians get women up fast and let them leave the hospital after three to five days.

Joan: Great, without my husband, what fun can the hospital be—if you get what I mean (wink - wink - wink).

Doctor: I think I do.

Joan: In plain language, how soon can sexual activity be resumed after having a baby?

Doctor: Well . . .

Joan: I guess it's best to wait until the anesthetic has worn off, eh?

Doctor: Plus six weeks. This gives the body time to heal and adjust.

Joan: After I have my baby, will I ever get my old figure back?

Doctor: With proper exercise, of course you will.

Joan: Damn it! My old figure was lousy. I want a new one.

Doctor: Your husband told me the same thing.

Joan: Now that I am about to become a mother—and I hope I'll always be able to live up to the exciting challenge of that role—my thoughts turn to circumcision. Are you for it?

Doctor: Only for boy babies. But I advise it for almost all boys. Circumcision is an obvious aid to cleanliness, among other things.

Joan: I get depressed just thinking about them having to cut my poor little baby.

Doctor: Some women have periods of depression after giving birth. But the mood should pass quickly. These depressions have a physical rather than psychological origin. During pregnancy the system of the mother is flooded with hormones which disappear right after the baby's birth.

Joan: Very often along with the baby's father! Now I am depressed and panicked about taking care of my baby at home. How will I know when he's hungry or whether he's too warm or cold?

Doctor: Babies are tough. They don't break. Think of all the mothers down through history who have given birth without the benefit of doctors or the benefit of hospitals.

Joan: Or the benefit of clergy! Anyhow, I'm scared to be alone with the kid. I mean, we hardly know each other.

Doctor: Being alone with your baby is not a frightening experience. All you need is a little common sense, concern for the baby's welfare, and lots of love. All your baby will want for the first few months is to be warm, full and dry.

Joan: Big deal! That's all I want!

Doctor: You'll be able to cope with your baby, I assure you. If you can get a helping hand from someone the first few weeks your baby is home, that's all to the good. But make sure that hand is peeling the potatoes and dusting the furniture instead of handling the baby. That's your job.

Joan: But how about a lady that could do both?

Doctor: Fine, if she's a visiting nurse who likes to do housework. But that's not a very probable combination.

Joan: You have to watch out for some of these visiting nurses. They sometimes get confused about who they're supposed to be nursing. A friend of mine caught her husband with their nurse. He claimed she was just showing him how to burp their baby. My friend was furious. She told her husband, "Get off her shoulder."

Doctor: Maybe your friend's husband was starved for affection. Often the husband feels left out. Even though he may be very interested in the new addition to the family, it may be that a glance a day can very well satisfy his curiosity. Remember, you and the child have been keeping company all these months. Daddy may be frightened by something so tiny and fragile.

Joan: That was his excuse on our wedding night.

Doctor: It could have been yours, too. I beg your husband's pardon, Miss Rivers. Was your wedding night a dud?

Joan: Was it! It was such a dud we postponed the marriage for four weeks. But it was mostly my fault. On my wedding night I should have known better than to wear a nightgown with feet.

Doctor: I hope you're a little more adroit in knowing how to dress the baby. Because your husband is going to learn by watching you.

Joan: If that's the case, the kid is in double trouble. I can't see my husband changing a diaper that has anything in it. And if it doesn't have anything in it, why change it?

Doctor: It is true that if diaper-changing were the test of a father's love, probably most dads would be found wanting in fatherly love. Now's the time when you've got to get your husband in the habit of sharing the workload. The best suggestion I have is that when you're ready to leave the hospital, you plan the trip home so that you, your husband and the baby are alone together. It may be the first time.

Joan: The way things happen these days it may also be the last.

Doctor: Of course, he won't be able to help you if you plan to breast-feed.

Joan: Do you believe in breast-feeding?

IF YOUR CHILD HAS A TENDENCY TO THROW UP AFTER MEALS, ALWAYS SEAT HIM NEXT TO PEOPLE YOU HATE

Doctor: I do, indeed. But only for babies.

Joan: I read somewhere that breast milk is for babies and cow's milk for calves. What's the difference, besides the containers they come in?

Doctor: Although mother's milk is excellent, today cow's milk has been adapted so that it is perfectly okay for babies to drink it. Most formulas try to copy breast milk.

Joan: Then the bottle's as good as the breast?

Doctor: No! There are still many pluses in breast-feeding. Chief among these are fewer digestive upsets for baby. Less spitting up. Less diarrhea. And no constipation. And perhaps a feeling of closeness that's hard to find in a bottle.

Joan: Try explaining that to a bankrupt dairy farmer's wife.

Doctor: Well, allergies seldom develop as they sometimes do with cow's milk. Also, a breast-fed baby has fewer skin rashes.

Joan: He also gets used to crowds earlier—if the mother decides to feed him in public!

Doctor: Breast-feeding is great for the mother. It helps the organs involved in birth return to normal very quickly. And it's a great way for you and your baby to get to know each other!

Joan: What if a mother decides she doesn't want to breast-feed?

Doctor: As I said, cow's milk today is prepared so that it's perfectly nutritious and free of germs. While you're giving him his bottle, you can also give him all the loving, cuddling and fondling he needs for his emotional security. And there should be no guilt. Not all mothers were meant to breast-feed.

Joan: What if you're all revved up for breast-feeding and the baby doesn't want to eat?

Doctor: Don't be dismayed if this is the case the first few days. At the same time, you may have no breast milk at the start, only colostrum. Within twelve hours after your breast milk comes in, you'll find baby taking a lively interest in his feed.

Joan: Do babies automatically take to nursing? I'd hate to have the baby reject me the minute it sees my breasts. It would bring back such awful memories of high school.

Doctor: Babies sometimes need some directing. You can help by holding the baby so his mouth can reach your nipple and by helping him to take the brown circle behind the nipple in his mouth, as well as the nipple. This will keep the nipples from becoming sore. Be sure to hold your breast away from his nose so he can breathe easily.

Joan: I guess that's where the expression "Smother Love" came from.

Doctor: There are other manifestations of "smother love," which we can go into later.

Joan: Is breast-feeding idiot-proof? I mean, is it possible to flunk the course?

Doctor: Occasionally a mother does fail, even after she's followed all the directions. But she hasn't failed her baby, and she shouldn't blame herself. Attitude has a great deal to do with success in nursing. It's been demonstrated that mothers who don't really want to nurse seldom have enough breast milk.

Joan: I don't know, Doc. How smart is a newborn kid, really? I think I'll keep my kid on formulas. He won't know the difference. I'll just take his bottle and shove it into my bra. I'm afraid with all that nursing I might become "The Sensuous Mother of the Year."

Doctor: Yes. Nursing is very pleasurable to both mother and child, even though it may hurt at first to have the baby tugging at your nipples. But they toughen up soon enough.

Joan: How long should the kid nurse?

Doctor: Only two to five minutes at a time for the first few days.

Joan: Should he alternate faucets, so to speak?

Doctor: In the beginning, yes. Later one breast per feeding can feed longer. Remember to soap your nipples clean and free of infection and to wash your hands before you touch them.

Joan: What position should I take when nursing—besides hiding in the closet?

Doctor: There is nothing to be ashamed of. Nursing is a wonderful and natural thing. So come out of the closet—or at least while you're in it, clean it—and choose whatever position is most comfortable and relaxing for you. Sitting in a rocking chair listening to the radio is very popular.

Joan: Yes. But some positions are bad for the mother. A friend of mine, a Yoga disciple, liked to nurse while standing on her head. It was great for the baby, but she was rather well endowed and ended up with two black eyes.

Doctor: That joke wraps it up for today. Make sure the nurse sees you on the way out.

Joan: Why?

Doctor: She can always use a good laugh.

CHAPTER V

Out of Those Girdles—and over the Hurdles!

The minute I had Melissa, Edgar started to complain. "Why can't you look like you looked on the day we got married?" he would rant. "Because I'm no longer pregnant," I'd yell back. But he was right. After the baby you should do some exercises to get back into shape.

Once Melissa was born I got busy right away with exercising. The most delightful "after-birth" exercise I found was opening presents, but the easiest was just to lie on my back and contract my tummy muscles in and out.

Once I got home my doctor told me when I could begin strenuous exercises such as this one for the tummy: Lie down on the floor, raise your legs together until they're straight up, then slowly lower them to the floor to the count of 40. If you like, put on a record or the radio to keep you company.

Many women like to do the exercises on TV, others prefer the floor. Either way is okay. Just remember, the only way you can get back to your old shape is by hard work. Avoid all those masseurs who promise to take five pounds off of you at each visit. The five pounds you'll lose will be your purse.

For the new mother, like everyone else, walking is the best all-around exercise. I really made it into a fun activity, as each day I set a goal for myself—like Tiffany's or Cartier's.

My doctor told me when I was able to rejoin my gym class that weight-lifting can be great for bust rehabilitation. But take care. Avoid the mishap of one poor absentminded woman in my class who was trying to get her bust back in shape in a hurry. By mistake she picked up two weights and worked out with them vigorously, completely unaware that one of them weighed five pounds and the other ten. Since then she's been known as "the odd couple."

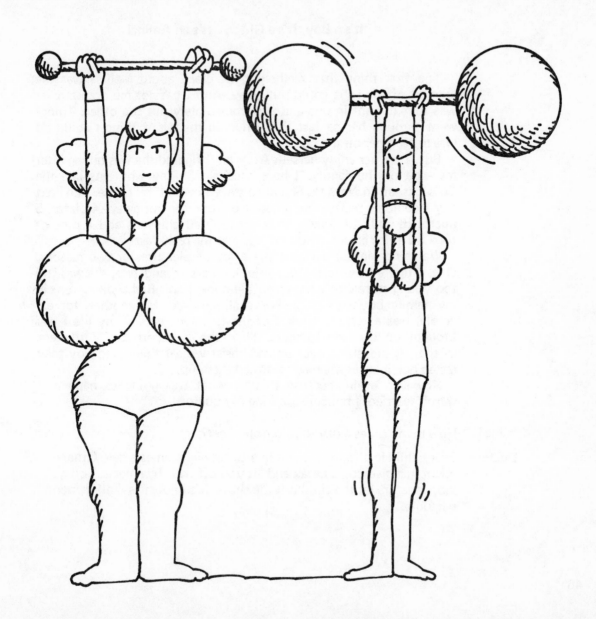

CHAPTER VI

It's a Boy, It's a Girl . . . It's an Animal

The first thing that really got me crazy about Melissa was the amount of food she could put away. And what got me even crazier was that it went in one end and immediately out the other. Things went through her so fast that I figured the wisest thing I could do was to feed her on the potty.

But, I let her enjoy herself. After all, I figured she was taking after my side of the family. I have a cousin Shirley who eats like the Cossacks are in Newark. She once stayed over at my house. The next day I couldn't believe the amount of food she put away—4 pizzas, 5 quarts of milk, 2 loaves of bread, 2 fried chickens and a pint of tutti-frutti ice cream. And that was just for breakfast!

Watching Melissa eat gave me a lot of pleasure for two reasons. One, I figured she really was enjoying herself, and two, she was still too young to realize what a terrible cook I am. Bad cooking runs in my family but who cares? We've all survived. My mother, for example, was a terrible cook. For the first ten years of my life I was brought up on radio dinners. Then she switched to TV dinners. Mother would stand over us and insist we eat them, and boy they tasted horrible—as she never warmed them up.

However, again, because I knew what was going to happen, I wasn't worried. I remember asking my doctor . . .

Joan: How many times a day should a child eat?

Doctor: Every child is different. Some like to eat eight times a day. Others might just give you a break and let you off with five meals. Today, most doctors let the child call the shots. It's known as "self-demand" schedule.

Joan: What does that mean? That my kid won't have regular meal times?

Doctor: Relax, relax, Miss Rivers. No child should be force-fed. Stuffing a baby is no way to demonstrate love. He should eat when he wants to. Adults jump the gun on mealtimes if they're hungry. Haven't you been hungry and grabbed a snack when you really shouldn't have?

Joan: Yes. On my wedding night. A lot of couples eat hors d'oeuvres after they've made love. I ate mine instead.

Doctor: I'll bet your husband was upset.

Joan: I'll say. I ate all the filled ones.

Doctor: Try to feed your baby in a nice, quiet atmosphere and try not to have any interruptions. That way you'll make a friend of him, and he'll think the world's a friendly place.

Joan: And what an idiot he'll grow up to be!

Doctor: I hate to detect this note of cynicism in you, Miss Rivers.

Joan: It's not a note, it's a scale. I was born and raised in New York where not too many people are friendly. Taxi drivers go right past you and give you the peace sign. Or half of it.

Doctor: Well, the world can be a warm and friendly place for babies if we just try to take care of their needs sensibly and with love. For example, they eat for two reasons. One, because they are hungry, of course. Two, because they love to suck. So give them a long enough time at each feeding to enjoy themselves or they will take their cravings out on something else. Like a thumb. And remember, stop several times during each feeding for a burp.

Joan: What if I don't want to burp?

Doctor: Not you, you idiot. The baby. Remember to burp him. This will help prevent indigestion or colic. Also, if the baby's crying an hour or so after his last feeding, chances are he is feeling a little indigestion, so pick him up and burp him, or try giving him a couple of ounces of water.

48

Joan: How about some milk mixed with club soda?

Doctor: No way, but you might try a pacifier. They help satisfy the baby's need for sucking.

Joan: Doctor, somewhere I read that most babies require a 2 a.m. feeding. This upsets me as that's usually the hour I'm coming in and I don't like to get pablum on my spangles.

Doctor: Cheer up. If that baby is halfway reasonable, somewhere between his third and seventh week he should be snoozing through until 3 or 3:30 a.m.

Joan: Great! That's when my husband gets in. And he doesn't mind getting pablum on his spangles, but he might object to getting something else on them.

Doctor: I presume, Miss Rivers, you are referring to the baby's bowel movements. Just don't be dismayed if there are no BMs the first day.

Joan: Dismayed! I'll be dismayed when they start coming.

Doctor: If the baby is breast-feeding, you can expect several movements a day, maybe one after each nursing.

Joan: Doctor, you have just made the most eloquent argument for bottle-feeding I ever heard.

Doctor: The bottle-fed baby usually has between one and four movements a day. Either way, the movements should decrease in number after the first month or so.

Joan: This morning on the radio I heard a golden oldie: "Every Little Movement Has a Meaning." Do you suppose some baby inspired that song?

Doctor: As far as your baby is concerned, every little movement means things are okay. Don't get uptight about any changes in color or frequency. But, if the consistency of the stool changes drastically, you should tell the doctor.

Joan: In other words, I'll have to be a stool pigeon for my own kid!

Doctor: Absolutely. Watch his stool carefully and also how he is passing it. Frequency of movements is no gauge to constipation. A baby is constipated when his stool is so hard he can't pass it without straining, or when it comes out in little balls.

Joan: How does one treat constipation in a baby?

Doctor: No laxatives and enemas unless prescribed by your doctor. A little more water or sweetening in the formula should loosen up the situation. If not, there's our old friend, prune juice. Maybe a tablespoon or two of the juice or prune pulp.

Joan: Then there's the other end of the rainbow....

Doctor: Diarrhea? Cut down on the sweetening in the formula. If it persists, you may have to cut out all food, especially fruit juices. A little boiled water, weak tea, or diluted, boiled skimmed milk at frequent intervals should help solidify things.

Joan: This whole discussion, as I see it, points in only one direction. Toward a pile of diapers about as high as the Empire State Building.

Doctor: I must say, you're a woman of remarkable perspicacity.

Joan: Only when it's warm outside and I've been very active.

Doctor: The point is, until baby is trained you are going to have to change a lot of diapers unless you want a diaper rash on your hands—

Joan: On my hands! My God, I can get a rash just by touching the diaper? Now I'm ready to believe you really can get syphilis off a toilet seat.

Doctor: If you want to keep the baby from getting a diaper rash, you had better change him before and after a feeding, after every bowel movement, or when he might be uncomfortable because of a wet diaper.

Joan: I'll be so busy changing the baby I won't get time to change myself.

Doctor: You can do that when the baby's asleep. Let him snooze even if he's wet, unless he wakes up and cries. And be sure you clean him thoroughly every time you change him. A good thing to use is sterile cotton, sterile water and soap. Then pat dry with a fresh towel, powder him thoroughly, especially in all the little crevices, and then put on a fresh diaper.

HAVING A BABY REALLY TAKES A LOT OUT OF YOU

Joan: What should I do with the soiled diapers? Send them to the cleaners?

Doctor: No, and your regular laundry won't take them either. You'll have to wash them yourself in your automatic washer at home. Or better yet, sign up for a diaper service that fetches and delivers. Or else try using disposable diapers.

Joan: Maybe my parents can help me?

Doctor: Usually grandparents are very helpful. The baby often gives them a whole new lease on life. But don't let them or the baby disturb your routine. Try to keep the routine of your house as normal as possible. If you start out tiptoeing around and shushing everybody, your baby will grow up thinking the only normal environment is a Christian Science Reading Room.

Joan: Listen, what happens if my folks or Edgar's hang around too much and try to take over the handling of my child?

Doctor: Put your foot down from the start. Remember, the child should have only one set of parents.

Joan: One visitor I'll be glad to see at any time is my father.

Doctor: Is there any special reason?

Joan: Because my father is a doctor and you know how doctors are. They hate to make house calls. The other night my father was called at 4 a.m. by a hysterical woman who wouldn't stop screaming. So finally, he had to get out of bed and get dressed and go. He figured if my mother was that upset, he'd better go home.

Doctor: Well, for the routine problems with your baby you may not need a doctor. Just consult a good baby book. If the answer isn't there, then call the doctor's office. Have a pencil and paper ready to take down whatever he says.

Joan: He usually says, "This will cost you $18, Miss Rivers."

Doctor: Your doctor will examine your baby very carefully before you leave the hospital. Then it shouldn't be necessary for you to take him back to the doctor for a month to six weeks for another checkup. At that time he'll set up a schedule for regular examinations. These routine visits are important as they will help your doctor get to know your baby intimately.

Joan: And if the doctor's cute, maybe they'll help me to get to know *him* intimately.

Doctor: Good afternoon, Miss Rivers. Next!

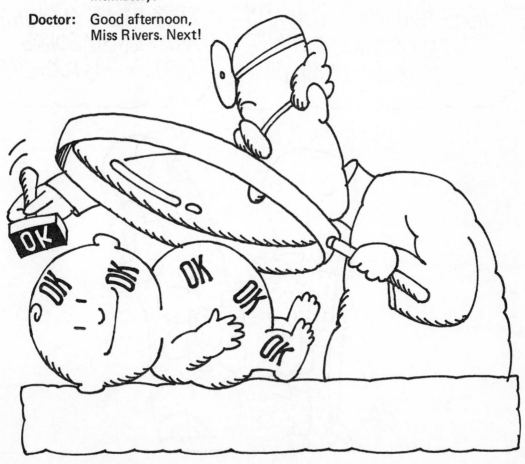

CHAPTER VII

Who Is This Stranger I'm Boarding? And Why Is He Making All These Impossible Demands on Me—and Never Once Has Said "Thank You"?

I think I can truthfully say I had no idea that motherhood involved so much work. If it wasn't changing the diapers, it was sterilizing bottles, or mixing formulas—and all that screaming, grabbing, crying and upchucking—finally, I told Edgar, "If you don't stop acting like this soon, I won't have any time for Melissa."

Yes, Edgar was jealous, and although I never told him, I was delighted because by the time I had Melissa, we had been married three years and a lot of his ardor had cooled. I mean the only way I could get him jealous pre-baby was to take his secretary out to lunch. And believe me, I tried everything. I left cigar butts in all the bedroom ashtrays, army boots under my bed and shaving cream in the bathroom. His only comment was, "Oh, is your Aunt Louise visiting us again?"

But now, suddenly all my time was being taken up by the baby—feeding, diapering, nursing, bathing, laundering, lifting, dressing, lullabying. Whoever said it is more blessed to give than to receive must have been a bachelor—or sterile!

I remember talking to my doctor about this. I said . . .

Joan: Listen, don't you think giving the baby a bath every Saturday night along with the rest of us would be plenty?

Doctor: I think once a day would be better.

Joan: What should I bathe him in? When I was a kid, my mother used a bathinette.

Doctor: Who are you kidding? When you were a kid, you were dunked in the village well. Anyhow, you can sponge bathe your baby on a table or in your lap. Or you can give him a tub bath in a washbowl, or a large dishpan, or even the kitchen sink—just make sure they are all scrubbed and rinsed out thoroughly beforehand.

Joan: Well, I can't use my kitchen sink. It's occupied all week until after Sunday dinner.

Doctor: With your dirty dishes?

Joan: No. With my maid. That's where she likes to sleep it off.

Doctor: Well, keep anyone who is not fully alert away from the baby at all times, especially during his bath when he is slippery and hard to hold. By the way, the best time to give the baby a bath is before you feed him. Afterward he'll be ready to sack out.

Joan: Don't I know it! I always take a nap after I've been fed. It gets them crazy in McDonald's.

Doctor: I'd get the bath out of the way before the husband and father get home.

Joan: Oh, that could never happen. They work on different shifts. And speaking of daddy coming home, how come a baby who has acted like an angel all day long suddenly sets up an unearthly howl at the exact moment when mommy chooses to fix herself up to look good for papa?

Doctor: It's called the "rush hour syndrome." The child senses the excitement and rushed preparations in the home before the father arrives.

Joan: Well, it isn't fair. Mothers should have time to fix themselves up.

SOAP

Otherwise, some husbands might start looking for a little extra-curricular activities. I mean, no man wants to make out with a wife wearing bunny slippers with one eye missing, an old terrycloth robe and toilet paper wrapped around her hair.

Doctor: Is that what Edgar told you?

Joan: Edgar? He was late himself twice last week coming home from the office. I got crazy. He claimed he'd been stuck in the rush hour traffic.

Doctor: Maybe that's really so.

Joan: But he works out of our den. Actually, that's good as he'll be around the house a lot and will be able to help me with the baby. I understand that there are a couple of areas of a baby's body that require special attention.

Doctor: And so do a couple of yours.

Joan: Okay, so I'm not in such great shape. I'm still grateful.

Doctor: For what?

Joan: That wrinkles don't hurt. Now, back to baby. What are the special areas?

Doctor: Well for one, caring for the penis is quite easy. You simply retract the skin with each bath to keep it from adhering to the head of the penis. This is especially simple to do if the baby has been circumcised.

Joan: And simpler, yet, if the baby's a girl.

Doctor: If the baby isn't circumcised, and you can't push the foreskin forward again, and the penis begins to swell, better call the doctor. Incidentally, don't be surprised to see your baby with an erection. This occurs commonly when the bladder is full or baby is urinating. Something else that might be swollen on both boys and girls is their breasts.

Joan: It should only happen to me. I'm so flat-chested. I bought one of those cross-your-heart bras. Instead of separating and uplifting, it sent out a search party.

Doctor: Sometimes baby girls bleed from the vagina, but there is no reason for alarm, as both this and the swelling of the breasts happen to infants because the mother's hormones pass through the placenta into the baby's bloodstream.

Joan: Was it Aldous Huxley who said, "Where the hormones, there moan I?" Any other special areas on my baby?

Doctor: The navel must be kept clean and dry. This means only sponge baths until the small cord drops off—which should be within three or four weeks, if not sooner.

Joan: My cousin Natalie got out of that little duty very nicely. She's been obsessed by how alienated kids are from their parents these days. So when she had her baby she refused to let the doctor cut the umbilical cord. "Time enough when he gets married, God forbid," she said. You never saw a closer relationship between a mother and son. They were inseparable. Of course, she found it tough to buy clothes.

Doctor: Speaking of clothes, when dressing your baby, less clothing is better than more.

Joan: That still is my theory—but I keep getting arrested.

Doctor: Mamas have always overdressed their babies and kept them bundled up no matter what the thermometer said.

Joan: You're telling me! One of the worst memories of my childhood is of the day my mother dressed me in a snowsuit, galoshes, stocking cap, scarf and mittens.

Doctor: Were you embarrassed?

Joan: And how. I was the laughing stock of the beach.

Doctor: A good rule to follow is: dress your baby as you dress yourself. If it is cool and you need a sweater, then so does he. Actually, a fairly plump baby needs less covering than an adult. Also, a variety of temperatures helps the baby to toughen up and become adaptable. You know, of course, how beneficial sunlight is to children and adults alike. Expose him to the sun just a little bit at a time. The ultraviolet rays give us all that good Vitamin D. Too much exposure can result in burns and injuries to his skin.

Joan: If mommy's a day over 30, she won't be caught dead in direct sunlight. I personally always wear a hat with a heavy veil and I tell my friends I'm raising bees. When should I take the kid out?

Doctor: By the time he's a couple of weeks old, the baby will be ready for his first buggy ride. That'll be a great occasion for both you and the baby.

Joan: And how. If I can find somebody to push us. Ah, problems, problems.

Doctor: Come now, things aren't so bad. Look at all the adults around you. Once they were babies, and they came through.

Joan: Yeah, but sometimes I think how nice it would be if my kid just slept for the first couple of years. Then, presto! Baby would awake when he's maybe three years old, with the frustrations and torments of being a baby all behind him.

Doctor: For the first few months he may sleep an awful lot. Most babies are up for various periods. Others may sleep almost every minute they're not being fed, changed, or bathed. But only your baby can tell you how much sleep he needs.

Joan: I've never been able to understand a thing any person under six months tried to tell me. I wonder if there's a course at the Berlitz School that would help.

Doctor: Even a heavy sleeper will cut down to a nap or two during the day as he gets a little older. But it's best to get an infant used to the idea that he goes to sleep right after he's been fed.

Joan: Well, then I'll have a problem. Who should I put to bed first, the baby or Edgar?

Doctor: You should also try to get him used to falling asleep in his own bed, without company. And don't wake him up to show to your family and friends.

Joan: If you ask me, many babies shouldn't be shown even when they're awake. A friend of mine had a kid who was really ugly. Once he fell in the gutter and the cop who found him called the ASPCA.

Doctor: After the first six months or so, the baby will probably give you a break in the morning by sleeping later.

Joan: Do you think with a lot of love and coaxing he could stretch that to noon?

Doctor: To 6 a.m., if you're lucky. But believe me, when you open your eyes and see him lying there on his tummy—

Joan: On his tummy?

Doctor: Yes. Most babies seem to prefer to lie on their tummies.

Joan: Which makes them smarter than a lot of mommies, who'd have been better off if they'd kept lying on their tummies.

Doctor: Incidentally, after six months, the baby should be moved out of your bedroom at night. When a child reaches that age, he's old enough to sleep on his own. Also, it's best not to take the baby into your bed at night for any reason.

Joan: No matter how helpless and frightened mommy might be feeling?

Doctor: Relax. Be cool. Have fun with baby.

Joan: Doctor, it was "having fun" that brought me baby. God knows what having more fun might lead to.

Doctor: You should let your baby know it's a joy having him. Talk to him and don't make caring for him a drag. You can be serious about being a good mother without being grim and tense about it. When the baby's awake, it wants companionship. But that doesn't mean you have to be its constant buddy. Sometime, let him help amuse himself. Give him things to play with that are safe. But remember that everything will end up in his mouth, so keep small objects that he can easily swallow away from him.

Joan: That's easy to do when he's in the crib, but what about when he gets older?

Doctor: Well, when you have the time to watch him, let him crawl around on his own and investigate his surroundings. But when you're busy, it's best to put him in a playpen. That way he can be where you are and see what you're up to.

Joan: Mommy's sometimes up to plenty she'd just as soon not have baby spying on. Besides, I've heard playpens aren't such a hot idea for babies.

Doctor: That's true. Many doctors feel that they keep a baby from becoming adventurous and exploring new territory, but the playpen can be a great boon, especially for the busy mother. When he's old enough to stand up, baby can hang on to the railing and feel the terra firma under him.

Joan: How can I help my kid get around before he starts to move on his own?

Doctor: A walker or a swing is a pleasant and useful device for the baby in that interval between learning to sit up and starting to creep . . . and speaking of creeps, Miss Rivers, your time is up.

CHAPTER VIII

If He Hollers . . . Let Him Go!

The only thing I couldn't get over with Melissa was the amount of time she spent crying. But when I say cry, I don't mean cry, I mean CRY. The last person I'd seen cry like that was Edgar on our wedding night. And it seemed like she would never stop and it really upset me. I mean, what has a baby got to cry about? It's amused and fondled and cuddled and bubbled and coo-cooed at all day long. If Edgar paid even half that attention to me, I'd give up kissing my pillow. I mean, how do you put a silencer on a squawk box? I tried everything to keep her quiet; I sang soothingly to her, I fed her, changed her diaper. Nothing helped. She just kept on screaming. Finally, I threatened that if she didn't stop crying, I'd never come near her again. That was the first time I ever saw Melissa sit up, laugh and clap her hands. And that started me crying! You know something, there's nothing like a good cry. I remember what my doctor told me . . .

Doctor: Babies cry because they're hungry or uncomfortable or need exercise. Again, the operative word is: Relax. You'll learn how to adjust the feedings to his needs.

Joan: Well, what if he's fed and still crying his head off, and I've already changed his diaper 13 times? There's nothing more to come out. Is the kid sick? Has he got a safety pin jabbing him somewhere I can't see? Can it be fatigue? How could it be when he's been on his back in his crib all day long? And it can't be loneliness either as mommy's been lying right there beside him.

Doctor: You may have a fretful baby. Try to find the cause. Or it may be just a stage.

Joan: The whole world's a stage. And we poor mothers are but stagehands. What should I do to stop the crying?

Doctor: Try wrapping the baby cozily in a receiving blanket. Maybe a pacifier between feedings. Or some music.

Joan: Great, and if none of these things work on me, I'll try them on the baby.

Doctor: If the baby screams its head off at about the same time every day, chances are the baby has colic. This usually comes after the feeding and is probably due to a cramping of the intestines. It's fairly commonplace. It too will pass. Don't panic. Remember, when you pick up the colicky baby to soothe him, he may scream harder than ever.

Joan: My mother was right. She loved to quote Shakespeare to my sister and me when we were growing up. Her favorite passage was from *King Lear:* "How sharper than the serpent's tooth is the thankless child!" Her dentist taught her that.

Doctor: If you get mad at the baby—and you will—just bear in mind the baby isn't consciously trying to bug you. He's just a little pile of parts and nerve endings and doesn't realize he's upsetting you. Admit you're mad and try to share a good laugh about it with your husband.

Joan: I'll have to find him first.

Doctor: Well, I can understand why you're tense, and the tension will only increase if you've got one of those real problemy, colicky, crying babies. You've got to think a little about yourself and your own sanity, too. Try to make some kind of arrangement where you can get away for three or four hours a day or at least twice a week, as every mother needs a relief shift—and her husband is as good a bet as any.

Joan: Or anyone's husband for that matter but, to tell you the truth, I don't really trust my husband with the kid. I think he'll try to spoil him.

Doctor: More often than not, it's the mother who does the spoiling.

Joan: Well, believe me, I won't spoil my kid. No fancy cars, or separate apartments—'til he's toilet trained.

SEYMOUR XAVIER SCHAINHOLZ, M.D.

Dear Joanie,

You are one busy girl! It seems every time I hear you on the Tonight Show you're getting ready to open in Las Vegas or Miami Beach or Chicago or wherever. It was lovely to hear that you take Missy and the nurse with you when you travel. You seem to be always on the go.

I can well imagine your mail has a hard time catching up with you-- and that a lot of it just plain gets lost in transit. So please forgive me for resubmitting my statement for bringing Missy into the world.

All best wishes for your continued success,

[signature]

Dear Joan,

I heard you joking the other day on the Merv Griffin Show about how inefficient your secretary is. You said you had dictated a letter that morning and the secretary asked you, "Does it have to get out this year?"

I can well imagine such a secretary is pretty sloppy about handling your mail. Who knows, she probably loses half of it and fails to bring the other half to your attention.

Therefore, please be understanding about my writing "Personal" on the envelope. You'll notice I didn't write "Urgent!" (ha, ha!) and that I took the liberty of enclosing a stamped, self-addressed envelope for you to use.

Most respectfully yours,

[signature]

67

Doctor: There are other ways to spoil a child.

Joan: By leaving him out in the rain and letting him rust?

Doctor: No. It could be that you've tried too strenuously to amuse your baby. If you have, the baby will be clamoring for fun and games from mommy all day long, and mommy will soon find the entertainment burden intolerable.

Joan: I've sometimes heard that same comment from my audiences.

Doctor: It's natural to spoil the first-born a little. Parenthood is a new game for mommy and daddy. The baby's the greatest thing that ever happened to them. They feel all this responsibility toward the helpless little bundle, and understandably they may overreact to the crying. But there are certain types who are more likely to spoil their babies. Take a person like yourself. Someone who's—what is the best way to put it—well, slightly older than springtime.

Joan: That was not the best way to put it. Besides, I'm 23.

Doctor: How can that be?

Joan: I don't count when I sleep.

Doctor: Because you waited so long to have your baby you might tend to give in to your baby's every demand. This is typical of older parents. You must stop and remind yourself that the baby doesn't have sense enough to know what's good for it.

Joan: Neither do I.

Doctor: Well, you'd better try and figure it out. And, frankly, if I were you, I'd enjoy this period now when you are the "boss" of your baby. Pretty soon, at about four years of age, he'll be questioning your every decision.

Joan: And probably winning.

Doctor: Ah—but only if you've let him win from the start. So don't let him. Just make up your mind that you're going to go about your normal routine most of the time your baby is awake.

Joan: That means I'll have to take the baby on the nightclub stage with me. Actually, it might be just the gimmick my act's been needing for a long time.

Doctor: Just don't turn him into a little tyrant of the night by letting him bully you with his crying. If you pick him up at night and start walking him when he sets up a howl, he'll have you walking all night long. Another cute trick a spoiled baby uses to command attention is to vomit when he gets into a snit.

Joan: Shouldn't a mother get worried? I mean, if I were doing it, I know my kid would be upset.

Doctor: Actually, vomiting and drooling and spitting up are common with babies. So just relax. Another thing many babies do is thumb-sucking. Everyone has a theory about it. Whether it's good or bad. Whether it should be tolerated or discouraged.

Joan: I'm against thumb-sucking. Only when everything else has failed and all entreaties to reason have been ignored, do I personally resort to it.

Doctor: A baby sucks his thumb mainly because he hasn't had enough of a go at the breast or the bottle to satisfy his sucking need. I think it might be an inherent trait that runs strong in some families and skips others altogether.

Joan: Well, it sure runs in my family. My cousin Shirley is 21 and is still a thumb-sucker.

Doctor: You mean to tell me a 21-year-old girl still sucks her thumb?

Joan: Not hers. Other people's. Poor thing. She goes crazy every time she sees a hitchhiker.

Doctor: Well, she's most unusual. Most thumb-suckers get started before they're three months old and usually phase it out by the time they're six or seven months old. If they're still sucking after that, they're doing it to soothe themselves and not to satisfy a sucking need. It's my own personal theory that a breast-fed baby is less likely to become a thumb-sucker. That's because his mommy will probably let him nurse to his little heart's content. But when a bottle's empty, it's empty, and baby doesn't get a big charge out of sucking air.

Joan: Listen, I've heard of many a baby that went straight from mommy's nipple to his own thumb.

Doctor: Then maybe his mommy should have let him nurse longer—a half hour or more if it's convenient.

Joan: It most certainly is not convenient. The way my day is programmed, I'd have to be nursing while I'm at the supermarket, cooking, cleaning, running errands, walking the dog . . .

Doctor: You could shorten that time if at each feeding you'd let it have both breasts.

Joan: At this point, I'd like to let it have both barrels. Is it true that thumb-sucking is bad for the teeth?

Doctor: A lot of parents worry about this and they really shouldn't, as long as the child has quit the habit by the time he's five or six years old when his permanent teeth are coming along.

Joan: My Aunt Helga looks like a saber-toothed tiger. Her teeth jut out so straight she can hang clothes from them. But then she's 48 and still sucking. At first her parents tried to stop her, but they couldn't. And besides, having prominent upper teeth has its advantages. She can walk in the rain and never get her chin wet.

Doctor: If you've got a thumb-sucker, don't be a nag. And avoid any restraints like mitts or putting icky stuff on the thumb. This will only frustrate him. Many mothers nip the thumb-sucking habit in the bud with a pacifier.

Joan: But you have to buy that. The thumb's cheaper. Another nice thing about a thumb is it doesn't keep falling on the floor. You don't have to keep sterilizing it, either. Besides, who wants to push a kid around who looks like it's got a corkscrew stuck in its mouth?

Doctor: The "plus" of a pacifier is that most babies will kick the habit when they're five or six months old. Whereas a thumb-sucker doesn't kick his until he's three or four years old or older. Besides the pacifier or thumb, when a baby is six months old he begins to reach for other comforters like his blanket.

Joan: And when he's sixteen, he reaches for who's under the blanket.

Doctor: A baby is about six months old when he first begins to realize he is a person in his own right and not just an extension of mommy. For some reason the other comforters that he picks—like a cuddly toy or diaper or blanket—are usually dirty. In fact, the dirtier and mangier the object, the greater can be the baby's devotion to it. There's really not much that you should do about it.

Joan: Except to put the kid and the comforter through a car wash once a month.

Doctor: The best thing to do is not to fight it. Try to clean the object, whatever it is, when baby's not looking. Or palm off a clean duplicate on him. But don't be surprised if he doesn't fall for the ruse. In any case, the child should give up this crutch, too, in good time.

Joan: Easy for you to say. My cousin Rebecca had an old blanket she adored. She carried it all over with her—even when she was grown up—and it caused a lot of comment. Maybe because it was a king-size electric job.

Doctor: Oh, one other thing that you should take in stride is any head banging or rocking in the crib.

Joan: But what if the baby is beating his brains out?

Doctor: Just pad the crib and don't get alarmed. The baby is just beginning to develop his sense of rhythm.

Joan: You're speaking of black babies, of course. I'm Jewish, so I don't have to worry. None of us have any rhythm. And neither do a lot of Catholics, from the sizes of some of their families.

Doctor: Well, take whatever rhythm you have and dance out of here.

CHAPTER IX

A Growing Baby May Be Hazardous to Mommy's Health and Nerves

As Melissa grew, I was delighted to see that she was bright—all things considered. I mean she was no genius like my sister's little boy who was so smart that when the rest of the kids sat in the sand box and made patty cakes, he made soil tests. But she wasn't a dummy like the kid next door who when she took her first step, took it backward.

The thing that I had to keep remembering was that each child is unique and has its own tempo. For example, Melissa didn't learn to eat with a fork 'til she was, say, past two, while my cousin's kid was less than eighteen months old when she first used her fork. The entire restaurant turned around to watch in amazement as such a young child—completely unaided—picked up her fork all by herself and stuck it into her new baby brother.

Of course, although I hated to admit it, one of the reasons I expected Melissa to be smart was because my family doesn't know from slow developers (outside of the girls in the chest area). My mother says I was the first kid on our block to put on her shoes and socks. Unfortunately, I put them on in that order.

Relax and let your baby develop his motor skills at his own rate. And once he gets such things as holding his head erect, sitting, standing, creeping and walking in that order, you can look forward to the next stage of development, which in Melissa's case included lighting my Tiparillo, tickling my back and refilling my Gatorade glass.

I still can hear my doctor telling me . . .

Doctor: There's little connection between a child's intelligence and how fast he acquires these skills. When we learn to stand, walk or whatever, our rate of progress has to do mainly with hereditary factors.

Joan: What about intelligence? Does that depend on heredity also?

Doctor:	Intelligence has more to do with environment, which is why I'm already worried about your child.
Joan:	How soon can you tell how bright a baby is?
Doctor:	Well, for the first two or three months the baby's almost totally wrapped up in himself.
Joan:	I know some babies who went on to spend the next 70 or 80 years being all wrapped up in themselves.
Doctor:	After about three months, he's ready to discover the world. In getting a grip on this little body of his, he starts by using his head.
Joan:	Doctor, you and I both know that's the last thing anybody ever uses.
Doctor:	Baby can tell light from dark the moment he's born. In a few weeks yours will be recognizing your face and responding to it.
Joan:	By screaming his bloody head off.
Doctor:	Keep smiling. He'll start imitating you. That's how he begins developing into a friendly, social being.
Joan:	Not by imitating my smile, I can assure you.
Doctor:	Gradually, after two or three months he learns how to use his hands, too, until he gets pretty good at it. Before he's a year, he'll dote on picking up the tiniest of things, like a speck of dust.
Joan:	Great! Then I can fire my cleaning lady. Doctor, I don't want to complain, but she is the worst. She swept so much dust under my rug, we have to walk uphill to get to the kitchen.
Doctor:	Miss Rivers, knowing your panic level, there's something I'd like to clarify. Parents tend to panic at the thought of a left-handed child. Which way the baby will go is not an inherited trait. He may go one way for awhile and then the other. A lot of babies straddle the fence for the first year or so and stay ambidextrous.
Joan:	And 21 years later, they're AC/DC?
Doctor:	The point is, do not force your child to use either hand. Let him use

the hand that is most comfortable for him—and the same goes with other skills. The age at which a baby learns to roll, sit up, stand up, and walk varies a lot. Temperament and weight have much to do with it. A fat baby may not have much of a yen to get moving very fast.

Joan: Don't I know it. I was such a fat baby I had barely reached the sitting up stage when it was time for me to go to camp. My parents took me there in a U-Haul-It. And by the time I got married, I was so fat, they had to roll me down the aisle.

Doctor: But you're so thin now, how did you accomplish that?

Joan: I just eat my own cooking.

Doctor: Well, if your baby does the same, he'll probably be thin and an early mover. Babies start creeping any time between six months and a year. But some never creep at all. They just sit around until they're ready to stand up.

Joan: I'd just as soon that any child of mine skipped the creep phase.

Doctor: A hot-shot baby might start walking at nine months. Most babies start between a year and 15 months. But many an intelligent, healthy baby doesn't take a step until he's 18 months or more.

Joan: If he was really intelligent, he'd put it off a lot longer and keep conning mommy into hauling and pushing him.

Doctor: Some mommies are apt to force the walking issue, and this is a big mistake. The baby will start to walk when it's good and ready to, without any parental prodding.

Joan: So I shouldn't try to help the baby by putting training wheels on him?

Doctor: Mothers who try to force their children to walk before they are ready can actually delay progress. Or mothers who "help" the baby to walk by constantly holding his hands and sort of swinging him across the room are really not helping him learn. This kind of sub-sidized walking can become too much fun for the baby to drop for the real thing.

Joan: Does the same apply to talking?

Doctor: And how! If there's any pressure on a baby to get talking, he may just decide to clam up. Usually, when babies are about a year old they are just making sounds that mean something—not actually words.

Joan: When should a mother start to panic?

Doctor: It's hard to say. When a child really begins to talk is mostly a matter of personality. An extrovertish type wants to get his two cents' worth in early. But the strong, silent type may take a long, cool look at the world around him before feeling any utterances coming on. Also, talking at the clip of a tobacco auctioneer as you do, Miss Rivers, your baby may have trouble being able to copy single words. Slow down. One word at a time.

Joan: And if the word keeps coming back to you as "grr" or "kl-kl," at what point do you really know you're the proud mother of a stupid child?

Doctor: You can't use speech as a gauge. Some very bright children don't talk much before three. Try not to get tense about it. Talk to him in a friendly way, using simple words, and try to coax him into asking for things by their name.

Joan: In other words, if my kid wants me he should call me, "Miss Rivers"?

Doctor: Your kid is going to want you a lot during teething, but you can't win any superiority sweepstakes because your baby teethed early. It proves nothing. The timing has to do with the baby's rate of bodily development.

Joan: I've always been told you can use it as an all-purpose cop-out. Your baby's screaming 24 hours a day and he throws up on Grandma anytime she picks him up. You just say, "He's teething."

Doctor: Too many things are blamed on teething that shouldn't be.

Joan: Like my wedding night.

Doctor: The average baby gets its first tooth around six months and continues teething for most of his first two and a half years. In that time he will get 20 teeth.

Joan: That's the same rate that I'm losing mine. Every time I hear the song "Bridge Over Troubled Waters," I think it refers to me.

Doctor: Much as it might disturb your aesthetic or hygienic sense, reconcile yourself to the fact that the baby's going to be chewing on everything it can get into its mouth.

Joan: Well, if it's chewing on mommy, it'll be chewing the fat.

Doctor: Better that he chew a rubber ring or something of the sort. And keep the baby away from thin celluloid toys and anything that's been repainted at home.

Joan: Thank God! That means my face is off-limits. Listen, Doc, what gives a child good teeth? I had bad teeth from the start. I lost so many teeth at once when I was a kid, the tooth fairy got a hernia.

Doctor: It depends a lot on what the mother ate during pregnancy, and the diet the baby is on after birth.

Joan: When do my baby's permanent teeth start forming?

Doctor: Just a few months after birth. Though they don't start putting in an appearance until he's six years old.

Joan: And I'll bet the dentists can't wait. I know my dentist made a fortune on me.

Doctor: The best way to avoid cavities is to avoid sweets. They really are the diggers of holes in children's teeth. If it's humanly possible, try to keep sweets away from your baby.

Joan: It's easier said than done. What kind of a mother can resist her kid's tears and won't share her lollipop or licorice stick with her own flesh and blood? I mean, I've even seen my dentist's wife slipping his kid candy.

Doctor: I'm truly surprised at that.

Joan: Well, they're a strange couple. We once went out to dinner with them. As soon as we sat down, he clipped my napkin around my neck, shoved two little cotton hot dogs in my mouth and when my martini came, he made me take a sip, swirl it around and spit it out!

CHAPTER X

The First Year Is the Hardest—Until the Second Year

I never thought I'd say it, but by the time Melissa reached one year I began to realize that when a mother referred to "the good old days," she was talking about her baby's first few months. All that happened then was Melissa ate, slept, smiled and screamed, and I was in control.

Then came her first birthday and it was all over. She wanted to go poking into everything, try everything, investigate everything. For all normal babies suddenly turn into explorers and nobody can tell them they aren't Marco Polo, Magellan, Christopher Columbus and Edmund Hillary combined—except maybe their psychiatrists when they're 21!

So, I had to let Melissa go, for nothing I could do or say could dampen her sense of adventure. Pulling, pushing, feeling, kicking, she simply had to put her touch on everything, and that was healthy. One can be a dangerous age (but then so can 17, if you cross a state line). To make my house safer I took a whole series of commonplace precautions.

I put harnesses on highchairs and in Melissa's carriage. Guards went on all the upstairs windows and in front of the stairs. Luckily I didn't have to take special care to keep Melissa from getting burned in our kitchen. She never went near it. She hated my cooking so much right from the start that at ten months she taught herself how to phone Chicken Delight. So be careful. I remember my doctor's first words of caution to me . . .

Doctor: Keep far out of reach all tiny objects like buttons, beads, peanuts, beans, pins, etc., that the baby might put in his mouth and which could get lodged in his windpipe.

Joan: Something really teensy-tiny, though, might go right down? Like the diamond on mommy's wedding ring?

Doctor: Electric cords should be in top condition. And outlets that are not used should be plugged up so baby won't be tempted to jam things into them. Keep dangerous tools out of sight. Matches also should be kept out of baby's reach. Swimming pools and wells should be fenced off. Put a life jacket on the baby whenever he's near water, and a safety belt on him when he's in the car. Keep him from being exposed to anything with a cutting edge. Opened tin cans, broken glass—

Joan: . . . his Grandma's tongue.

Doctor: Used razor blades should go back into their container.

Joan: That's a great excuse for me to stop shaving.

Doctor: Go through your house from stem to stern and tuck everything away that's potentially poisonous. All medicines and insecticides and cleaning materials and polishes and sprays and detergents and rat poisons and gasoline and kerosene and turpentine and the like. Be sure to put all pills safely out of reach. Babies seem to have a special yen for pills—maybe because they see you take them and want to imitate mommy.

Joan: Because of this my cousin gave up the pill. She practiced the rhythm method for five years and ended up with four kids who are great tap dancers.

Doctor: This is the age when a baby might be both frightened and fascinated by strange objects that make sudden loud noises, like trains or planes or the whirring of a blender or a power lawnmower or the barking of a dog. Shield him as best you can from these disturbances. If the running of a vacuum cleaner should frighten him, give up using it in front of him for a few months.

Joan: If the running of the vacuum cleaner doesn't frighten him, what measures can I take to see that it does?

Doctor: Also, at this age, the bath can suddenly become terrifying. If a tub frightens him, use something smaller, like a dishpan, or get special toys for the bath. There are special soap crayons most children like, as they can paint themselves and get cleaned at the same time.

Joan: All kids I know love their baths. My sister's little boy giggles and laughs from the time she puts him in the washing machine until he's spun dry.

Doctor: Remember, this is the time for letting the baby try his wings. His journey to freedom and independence begins with a crawl—all the way to another room. Soon he can walk, and when he can walk, don't keep him secured in his carriage. He needs his daily constitutionals. Don't let him wander off and put sand and dirt in his mouth, of course, but it's perfectly healthy for him to get dirty.

Joan: With all this crawling and walking, I guess it's bye-bye playpen?

Doctor: Yes, now it's going to be hard to keep him out of trouble and in the pen. And pretty soon you're going to have to let him have the run of the house.

Joan: Hey wait a minute, that's a prerogative my mother still doesn't let me have. To this day I've never been in her living room. I just stand at the entrance and admire it over the rope.

Doctor: Your mother was probably afraid that you'd break things. You can prevent this . . .

Joan: By handcuffing the child . . .

Doctor: By putting the really rare and lovely things out of his reach and putting interesting alternatives in their places. Besides, a child of one can be taught not to do certain things such as touch a hot stove, turn on the gas, pull lamps off the tables by their cords . . .

Joan: . . . or wake mommy before noon.

Doctor: Just get ready to say "no" over and over and say it like you mean it, firmly but cheerfully. Also distract him if you can with something allowable that he's apt to find as interesting as the forbidden object.

Joan: If laryngitis starts coming on before those thousand no's are said, how about one giant "Bug off"?

Doctor: Blowing your cool will accomplish nothing. Yelling, scolding, dirty looks, finger waving will not do the job. He'll either have to give in meekly or go on defying you.

Joan: What's wrong about giving in meekly? After all, "Blessed are the meek for they shall inherit the earth." A probate judge told me that.

Doctor: Bullying a baby into submission is bad for the development of his personality. So control yourself. You'll have to prevail, but do it in good humor, without arguments or scoldings, no matter if he kicks and screams his bloody little head off. Deep down, he'll feel good knowing that you're doing what has to be done without getting mad.

Joan: It's hard being a mother.

Doctor: It's harder being a baby. Think how big everyone and everything looks to him—and how frightening it must be when visitors swoop down and try to hug and kiss him. Babies need time to size up strangers before getting chummy. Often when people pounce on the baby, he'll cry and retreat back to mommy. When this happens, just say, "The baby's a little bashful."

Joan: But mommy's not bashful and would love to be pounced on.

Doctor: Something else you'd better be prepared for is the time when the baby starts dropping things. Not to bug you. He's doing this dropping and throwing on purpose because it's a big new achievement for him. He'll be pleased as anything to have you returning the things to him. That makes it a two-person game, but it's best not to make a habit of picking up the things he's dropping.

Joan: But won't the Board of Health have something to say about that? I mean, with the piles of mashed bananas and wet cereal and boiled eggs mounting up on my floor?

Doctor: I was referring to his toys. When a baby gets into a dropping mood, put him on the floor. Or tie his toys to his pram or his highchair with short pieces of string.

Joan: What if he starts throwing his food? My friend Mary's kid did that, but she didn't get mad. She knew he was just imitating his father.

Doctor: A baby won't start throwing his food 'til he's pretty full. At this point take the food away and just let him play. And by the way, it's at this age he'll start getting much choosier.

Joan: I know. Mary told me. Once she had prepared a great meal for her kid—lamb chops, spinach, mashed potatoes and ice cream—and he wouldn't touch it. She was so upset. It had taken her hours to stuff all that into the bottle.

Doctor: At one, a baby often isn't as hungry as he was. Teething may have something to do with it. So don't force-feed. He's entitled to his personal preferences in food. From the start, try to act sensibly about feeding and you won't have problems later on. Get across the notion that eating is enjoyable.

Joan: In my house that will be easy. I'll just smile and say, "Eat some more, honey. It's good. Mommy didn't make it."

Doctor: As long as you're offering a good selection of wholesome foods, don't worry about how much or how little he may eat at one meal. Or if he seems to be addicted to avocados one week and won't touch them the next. And if your child is a poor eater, games will help distract him.

Joan: My father used to play airport with me. The food was the plane and my mouth was the hangar. He'd say, "Here comes the airplane into the hangar." I loved that game. I even made up my own version. It was called "Spit the airplane in the pilot's eye." When will my baby be able to feed himself?

Doctor: That depends mostly on the parent's attitude. Some babies can do a pretty good job of spoon-feeding themselves before they're a year old. Then you'll hear a certain kind of mother say that her two-year-old couldn't conceivably feed himself.

Joan: Well, we all know what kind of a mother that is. She and her darling little Herbie will be spooning together down through the years.

Doctor: A baby can take his first step toward self-feeding when he's only six months old and he's allowed to hold some finger foods.

Joan: In my house, all foods are finger foods. I figure, if God wanted us to use utensils, our hands would be silver plated.

Doctor: 'Twixt the spoon and the lip there's many a slip, however. The baby who thinks that if his parents can use a spoon he surely can is in for a rude surprise. The first few hundred tries he'll find that for every particle of food that reaches his mouth, 99 others have fallen on himself or the floor. But don't help him out. Let him have a go at it. At the beginning of a meal, he'll be hungry enough to persist. The more adept he gets at feeding himself, the longer you should let him stick with it.

Joan: Until one meal just kind of blends into the next?

Doctor: He'll get so he can knock off something he really likes in ten or fifteen minutes. At that point don't start spoon-feeding him the other things he should be eating. In his young mind that will set up a distinction between what he wants and what you want to get into him. And by all means don't fret about table manners. Believe me, the baby wants to be neater and cleaner as fast as he can manage it.

Joan: Table manners worry everyone. Which fork to use with what? I have a rule, just start with the thing farthest away on your left and work in toward your plate.

Doctor: That sounds logical.

Joan: Except for the time I found myself trying to eat soup with a napkin.

Doctor: One last thing. About the age of one, your baby may be giving up his morning nap. The baby that snoozed so regularly at 9 a.m. may start putting off that nap until it runs into the lunch hour. In that case, serve an early lunch. Lunch will probably go immediately into a long nap.

Joan: All this talk of bed reminded me I have to return my water bed. I bought it strictly for sex, but my husband stocked it with trout. So long, Doc.

CHAPTER XI

There Is No Such Thing as Kiddy Litter

Once your baby has some teeth, is crawling about and is able to say a few words, it's the time (hooray) to housebreak him.

Every mother has her own method. Mine was the applause gimmick. Melissa and I got off to a great start with this. Every day I would put her on the potty and when she had done what I wanted I would applaud her efforts. Just like the books said, I did this for several weeks and I was beginning to feel quite confident. Then Melissa got things backward, and whenever the television was on and she heard applause, she went to the bathroom . . . in the living room.

A friend of mine who trains dogs tried to apply the same methods she used to her child. She used to hit him over the nose with a rolled up newspaper the same as she did with her puppies. But it didn't work out. By the time her baby was three, he still wasn't trained, although he had learned to fetch, beg and roll over.

I hate to brag, but Melissa learned very quickly. I'll never forget the day she was finally trained. It was quite an event. Not only did it mean the end of all the messiness and dirty diapers, but it even had a greater significance: it meant the end of my affair with the diaper man.

However, all this was a long time after my first discussion with the doctor about toilet training . . .

Joan: Tell me, Doc, when can I start training my kid? I trained the dog at two months.

Doctor: When your youngster is old enough to learn the hang of it and physically able to bring it off.

Joan: That's too bad. In my cousin Shirley's case it wasn't until she was 14.

Doctor: Some babies can sit on the potty in the latter part of the first year. The kind of baby to put there will be the one who usually has a BM a few minutes after breakfast every day. That way the mother can predictably "catch" his movement.

Joan: That's what I call a regular baby.

Doctor: You can't expect baby to be conscious of what's happening there on the toilet seat. But after a few weeks of this he may sense that the moment he gets the seat under him is the time to start pushing.

Joan: And may I have the pushiest kid on the block!

Doctor: This early start, as I said, can be all to the good. But the baby who is "regular" is cooperating unknowingly. Later, when he's wise to what's been happening, he may clam up and resist. But after the first year things start looking up. The baby becomes aware of his BMs, and he takes a possessive attitude toward them.

Joan: That's your definition of things "looking up"?

Doctor: And he'll be so proud of what he's done—whether it's in his diapers or in his potty. Sure as anything, he'll want to show it to mommy.

Joan: I can't believe my life. I'm bankrupting myself to buy flowers and art reproductions in order to create a truly beautiful environment for him, and the kid wants me to look at BMs.

Doctor: Soon after he's a year old, he'll go through a couple of phases that will indicate he's ripe for toilet training. Neither one will seem to be directly related to bowel movements—but they are. You'll notice that he becomes a very giving little person. For instance, if you have a friend who's visiting, he'll drag out all his toys and make presents of them to her. This shows his pleasure in parting with something and getting mommy's approval for a grown-up gesture. Then you'll notice how intrigued he gets with putting things into containers. He might also start alerting mommy with some special gesture or noise when he feels a movement coming on. When you do catch the movement, it's an occasion for rejoicing and congratulating the baby on acting like a big boy or big girl.

Joan: If he wants to act really grown-up, he'll learn how to be constipated.

Doctor: Be prepared for relapses during this period. The baby between one and one and a half years old who seems to have gotten the hang of using the potty may suddenly balk. He'll hold everything in as long as he's on the potty and let go the minute he's off.

Joan: I have an idea. I'll show him who's boss. I'll strap his little behind to the potty and say, "Now you're not moving until you move."

Doctor: That's precisely what not to do. Don't keep him on the potty more than ten or fifteen minutes at a time, regardless of the results. If nothing happens, don't let your frustration show, for by the second half of the second year most babies are aware that a BM is coming, and they'll actually notify you when the great moment is at hand.

Joan: Oh, how I long to hear those three little words.

Doctor: "I love you"?

Joan: No. "Gotta go potty."

Doctor: Up to the time he's maybe two or two and a half years old, the baby is probably better off on his own small potty chair than on a seat that fits on the toilet. He'll be able to mount his little throne without any help from you, and he'll be proud to have his own little piece of furniture. However, it's a good idea to wait until he's left the bathroom before emptying the potty into the toilet and flushing it.

Joan: Good heavens, you'd think the kid was Howard Hughes. You know he never goes to the bathroom. He's hired four faceless peasants to go for him.

Doctor: The reason for not flushing in front of the baby is that some babies get frightened by the sudden torrents of water. Don't introduce him to his potty cold turkey. Let him do some dry runs on it—let him get used to his potty just as if it were a new plaything. Let him have some fun, while sitting on it fully clothed. Then, subtly—or not so subtly—you can sneak in the commercial: "This is your very own potty in which you can go to the bathroom. Like big people do on the big toilet." And one fine day—

Joan: One fine day, baloney. Remember, Doctor, you can lead a baby to potty but you can't make him ca-ca.

Doctor: Nevertheless, by the time he's eighteen months old I think you should start trying, whether or not baby seems so inclined. Consider it your responsibility to—

Joan: I know—to make his business *my* business.

Doctor: Even at this stage a youngster is most apt to let mommy know *after* the fact. But cheer up. This is still a sign of progress.

Joan: You have the most perverse definitions of progress.

Doctor: While you're cleaning him up, keep telling him that there's a better, more grown-up way of doing things and that's to make them into the potty. During the second half of the child's second year, you'll get a boost from his natural inclination to imitate and please his parents.

Joan: An inclination that quickly passes, no doubt.

Doctor: If it's a first-born, he won't, of course, have a big brother or sister to watch. Most authorities seem agreed it isn't good for him to watch his parents on the toilet.

Joan: Together? I'll bet that's one even Havelock Ellis never heard of.

Doctor: He's not going to learn in a few days or even weeks, and you've got to be his patient, cheerful and optimistic guide.

Joan: I have a great idea. What if I keep him on a liquid diet 'til he gets the hang of it?

Doctor: Be a little firm when you think he knows what he should be doing and is stalling. But no nagging or sermonizing, and don't be above a little harmless bribery. Like promising some new clothes or a wanted dolly when the feat is accomplished.

Joan: So, that's why my husband's training is perfect.

Doctor: As soon as the baby can stay clean part of the time, you can get him out of diapers and into training pants. This is a big leap forward psychologically.

Joan: The only big leap forward I'm interested in is the one that lands him on the toilet seat in time.

Doctor: Then, voila! One happy day you find you can depend on baby to let you know when he's ready for action. But he still expects you to take down his pants and get him on the seat. He can do both these jobs for himself when he's about three. And he can begin wiping himself. By the time he's two and a half years old, he should be trying his hand at this, if you'll forgive the expression.

Joan: So far we've been talking just about BMs. I hate to sound show biz, Doc, but to quote the song: "Another opening, another flow."

Doctor: Urine training can be a tougher job than BM training.

Joan: Thanks, Doctor, I really needed that to complete my day.

Doctor: It seems to go slower anyway—especially for boys. Most two-year-olds have pretty much mastered BMs, but plenty of two-and-a-half-year-olds are still moist little people, because for eighteen months or so a baby's bladder flushes itself almost automatically. But then, one glorious day the mother discovers her baby has been dry up to two hours.

Joan: To think such happiness could be mine!

Doctor: But it's not because the baby's going into training. It's just that the bladder is maturing.

Joan: This is the time to hire a wet nurse, right?

Doctor: I suggest that you put him on the potty every two hours. His bladder should be full by then so he won't have to be enthroned too long. Place him there in the morning as soon as he wakes up, before and

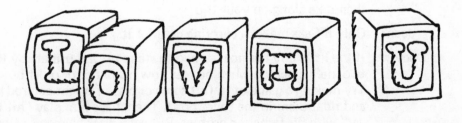

after naps and meals, and after he's been dry for two hours.

Joan: And sing him "Tinkle, tinkle, little star. . . ."

Doctor: Potty training is not an Olympic feat. There shouldn't be any sense of competitiveness with other children. Parents shouldn't compare their child's progress with that of other people's babies.

Joan: But what else do you talk about with other mothers? You're in that park and you hear some mommy bragging, "My little Suzy's only nine months old, but she's a perfect lady the way she takes care of her private functions." Well, you've just got to find a topper. Like, "My Johnny not only takes care of himself, but he helps his father zip up."

Doctor: Years from now, you won't be able to remember just how long it took. But it will matter if the training was carried out with love and patience and a bond of mutual trust was established between you and the baby at this time.

Joan: I was rather hoping the bond would come about through a shared appreciation of gourmet cooking, literature and good music.

Doctor: Incidentally the well-trained child of, say, two sometimes gets so conditioned to his own potty chair that he can't perform anywhere else. Again, when this happens, no nagging or scolding—even if he eventually wets his pants. If possible, condition your child to urinating in different places.

Joan: And all of them off the old reservation.

Doctor: Consider bringing along his own potty when you go traveling. There are also portable urinals which you can get him used to at home and then take along on your trip.

Joan: Only if Saks makes a carrying case for it.

Doctor: If the little boy has not learned to stand up and urinate by the age of two, he'll catch on when he sees how his father or older boys do it. Try making a game of it. Cut some circles of bright colored paper and float them in the toilet bowl. Then, have him play "hit the target" with his father or brother. But even after he seems to be trained, there are going to be "accidents" for one reason or another—stress or excitement or cold weather or a change of scene, etc.

Joan: I just hope my kid won't be accident-prone.

Doctor: And there will be times when training just breaks down.

Joan: And a time when mommy just breaks down.

Doctor: I think we've become unnecessarily self-conscious and uptight about toilet training. Curiously, many women who have read or heard next to nothing about child psychology in general and toilet training in particular often manage to do a job superior to their better educated sisters, simply by using common sense and following their own sound instincts. They aren't so likely to interpret temporary resistance as hostility. They just get on with it and stick to it. So hold to the line and be of good cheer.

Joan: I'm practically dancing on air. Oh, Doctor, on my way out, would you mind terribly if I used your bathroom?

SEYMOUR XAVIER SCHAINHOLZ, M.D.

Dear Miss R,

Please forgive me for writing you in care of your parents but several of my bills have come back marked, "Addressee Unknown."

I recall your once telling me that your father is a doctor also. I am sure he will be sensitive--and sympathetic--to the matter at hand and will take pains to see that this communication reaches you.

I hope all is well with you and little Melissa--or should I say, "big Melissa"?

Respectfully yours,

[signature]

P.S. I am enclosing an additional stamp to add to my return envelope as postal rates have gone up twice since I mailed it to you.

CHAPTER XII

If You're Giving a Party for One- or Two-Year-Olds,
Restrict the Guest List to Singles

Hard though it is to believe, before you know it your baby will be ready for fun, and your house will suddenly be loaded up with every kind of toy and gadget in the world.

Melissa was barely able to focus when our apartment started to look like Santa's workshop. Every room was filled with blocks, dolls, choo-choo trains, mobiles and woolly animals. It was driving me crazy, as now there wasn't any room left for my blocks, dolls, choo-choo trains, mobiles and woolly animals.

I was one of those mothers who liked to give children's parties at the drop of a rattle, and by the time I realized how much bother and trouble they were, it was too late. Melissa and I were in the social swing.

From all these parties I developed a fantastic knowledge of how to entertain children which I'd like to pass on to you. I also developed an ulcer which you can have, too.

I have found that my best parties were the ones that had a theme. Some of those used which worked well were "Balloons," "Candies" and "Tiny Toys." But don't let the children pick the theme, or it will be "Wreck the Joint."

I always used to start the party off with organized games such as musical highchairs, pin-the-diaper-on-the-donkey and spin the formula bottle. When these games got the little darlings too excited, I'd give myself a break with a game of hide-and-seek. I'd tell the little darlings to hide, and I never could find them until just before refreshment time. Then to save aggravation and trouble I'd serve the cake and ice cream right on the floor.

Whatever you do, however, keep the children busy. If the party gets too relaxed, the kids may let down their hair and break toilet training—and nobody needs party poopers around.

But don't let me leave you with the wrong impression. Children's parties can be fun—especially that supremely magical moment when

you hear yourself saying, "The party's over."

I have been saving my best advice for the last. If you really want to give your child a terrific party and save all the wear and tear on yourself, find another kid born on the same day—and persuade his mother to give the bash! Then at the end of the party, tell her she was a terrific hostess, toast her with champagne, get her smashed and take home all the expensive presents for your kid.

Doctor: Ah, but your little darling couldn't care less. Most babies prefer simple toys to the elaborate and expensive ones. The very best plaything for a one-year-old is a block that runs on wheels and has holes for pegs. Or a plain cardboard box with a string. First he'll enjoy pushing it. Then a little later he'll pull it around.

Joan: If he's all wrapped up in pushing and pulling, why can't I give him a mop?

Doctor: A baby also wants to be doing what mommy's doing. If she's cooking or putting dishes in the washer, then that's what the baby wants to be doing too, even if it's hard.

Joan: This mommy does something even harder than clumping around with pots and pans. She tries to knock five years off her face by putting on her eye liner, false lashes and eye shadow. Shadow, of course, is the hardest to put on as I never knew you had to shut your eyes.

Doctor: By the age of two, children become more creative. This is the time for all kinds of vehicles, dolls, doll houses and especially blocks. A big pile of blocks is worth a bagful of other kinds of toys you could give a child in his early years. With these he is able to be a creator. One important caution for parents is not to try to hurry a child into being logical and rational in his playing.

Joan: Particularly if the father isn't logical or rational in his playing around. My husband used to date such dogs, I wouldn't let them up on my couch.

Doctor: A mother of a baby girl, for example, might bring her baby daughter home a doll with a whole wardrobe for it. But when the baby dresses the doll, she puts on the coat first and the doll is wearing nothing underneath. Unless mommy is understanding, she might tend to get impatient.

Joan: Of course she might. The baby at this stage is supposed to be creative, and not still imitating mommy.

Doctor: Or if it's a boy, the father who's bought his baby son a model of the Super Chief complete with tracks can get upset when his darling heir takes the caboose and throws it against the wall. But it's asking too much to expect the baby to know that the whole train should go right on the tracks.

Joan: Especially if the old man's off his trolley.

Doctor: Suppose someone gives the baby a box of crayons and a coloring book. He has no concept of staying within the outlined shape of objects. His crayon brushes back and forth in every which direction. Nor can he be bothered with color differentiations. Mountains and trees and deserts and houses and people may all be rendered bright purple. Just don't be peeved with him for not painting the trees green and the deserts brown.

Joan: Peeved? I'll encourage him. If he keeps on coloring just like that he could grow up to become an Abstract Expressionist and con people into paying $50,000 for a painting.

Doctor: Just don't rush him or you'll make him feel inadequate when he can't live up to your expectations.

Joan: I know the feeling. That's how I felt the first time I went to buy a bra. The saleslady laughed and said I should come back in five years. I was twenty-four at the time and lonely. But then I never did have many friends. As a child I was so fat no one could get close enough to me to know I was fun.

Doctor: I'm sure that won't happen to your baby if you let him develop friendships early. Your little one will begin to seek out the companionship of his peers when he's one and a half or a little older. This can be an unnerving spectacle because no child of that age gives up his toys in the spirit of sharing.

Joan: I don't blame the kid. When's the last time you saw a daddy sharing his stocks and bonds or a mommy her jewels?

Doctor: The feeling of generosity will come to him—when he begins to have a real fondness for other children.

Joan: That feeling of generosity could come so gradually it might not show up till the next world. I never saw Howard Hughes or J. Paul Getty giving anything away.

Doctor: Don't force sharing on him before he's ready for it. It'll just make him clutch his possessions more firmly than ever, and he'll figure the world's a place where everybody's out to take everything away from him.

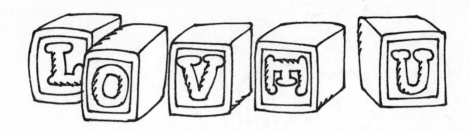

Joan: Do you really think he'll be smart enough to figure that out by the time he's two?

Doctor: When he starts getting a kick out of socializing with his young pals, you can make a little game of it: "Okay, first it's Jimmy's turn to make anything he wants out of the blocks."

Joan: ". . . then it's Tommy's turn to destroy it."

Doctor: When he first starts playing with other children, your first-born may find that the other kids are grabbing his toys away from him. But very soon he'll catch on and learn how to protect his turf and get back what's his.

Joan: And everybody else's, if he's going to grow up a winner.

Doctor: If some real bully keeps giving your child a hard time, then take him somewhere else where he can find other playmates.

Joan: Whom *he* can bully..

Doctor: Sometimes it's especially hard for the first-born to learn to share, as his parents tend to fuss over him. By the time the second one comes along, most parents have learned how to relax a little more and not overdo everything.

Joan: By the time the second one comes along it's amazing that they have the energy left to even *underdo* anything.

Doctor: After a while the child should be creating his own interests and meeting the world on his own terms. But if the parents are always anticipating him, picking him up, showing him off, and getting into a stew when he's sick or badly behaved, that baby's going to believe he's the brightest star in the whole solar system. He'll expect everybody to find him charming and lovable without his making any effort to be charming and lovable. And do you know how he'll end up?

Joan: As President of the United States?

Doctor: You should also be prepared for the fact that just about the time your child is beginning to frame whole sentences, he may take special delight in talking dirty.

Joan: I'll be upset only if I'm told to do something with myself that's physiologically impossible. My aim is to oblige any reasonable requests.

Doctor: If you appear either shocked or amused, your youngster will know he's on to a good thing and won't let go of it. If you're really put off by a dirty mouth on small fry, the best way to cope is not to react in any way. When you've had your fill, quietly say something like, "Those really aren't very nice things to be saying. And most people—even grown-ups—don't like to hear words like those."

Joan: . . . in the daytime, that is.

Doctor: That's a wild thing to say, Miss Rivers.

Joan: I know, Doc, but sometimes I can't control my mouth.

Doctor: That's due to aggressiveness—which in adults or small children, particularly boys, is one of the universal facts of life. Even our movies and television are filled with it.

Joan: I've always wondered why we needed to look at violence on the screen when we can find so much of it in the home.

Doctor: As far as toys are concerned, I'm against anything more warlike than water pistols, but trying to keep a child from owning or touching any war toys is easier said than done.

Joan:	Particularly when mommy keeps a loaded revolver under her pillow.
Doctor:	Probably the best approach is to quietly explain your disapproval of them. Without getting preachy, you can tell him that we must all learn to be kind and friendly to one another and not go around shooting people.
Joan:	Edgar and I couldn't agree more, and believe me we get this message across to all our friends by smacking it into them.
Doctor:	One thing on which I wouldn't budge is X-rating the murder and mayhem trash on television. I'd keep all the sadistic, savage bestiality strictly off-limits. It's definitely harmful for the small, impressionable child.
Joan:	That's the perfect argument for two television sets in every home! The parents can go on slaking their thirst for violence at the same time they're teaching their kids the joys of peace.
Doctor:	Another manifestation of aggression that can be a bother is the biting habit.
Joan:	I know, Doc, but I can't help myself. Sometimes I get so provoked that I think the only way the baby will listen to me is if I take a good bite out of him.
Doctor:	The baby who occasionally bites his playmates or his parents at this age but otherwise seems to be okay in disposition should not cause worry. If you're bitten, don't bite back or fly into a rage. At all times you must remain the benign boss. When you see those little teeth bared for action, calmly but pointedly get out of their way. He'll soon learn that it's a habit that's got to go.
Joan:	Something's got to go—either the habit or his teeth.
Doctor:	As far as playmates are concerned, they'll soon let him know how much he can get away with. When you see one youngster biting or punching another, it's a mistake to rush in and try to stop him.
Joan:	Sure. He might turn on me.
Doctor:	Leave him alone. He'll have to take his lumps from his victim, but if

mommy keeps interceding, he'll get the idea that it's okay to keep biting and slugging away as mommy will always come in time to protect him.

Joan: What if my kid turns out to be the muggee instead of the mugger?

Doctor: If your child's been on the receiving end and is really miserable or hurting, give him sympathy but don't overreact to his complaint. Look quickly for ways to distract him. Don't encourage weeping and whimpering over every little thing, but don't be afraid to be comforting. It won't make a sissy or a cry-baby out of him.

Joan: Unless he already is.

Doctor: At this age children don't differentiate between boy play and girl play. For example, no parent should be upset to see his two-year-old son playing with dolls. It is only when children get to be three or so that their sex identities sort themselves out, and boys and girls seek out activities normally associated with their gender.

Joan: Like "Let's play Doctor and Mommy." That would be okay, right?

Doctor: Right.

Joan: And I guess you'd only be in trouble if the little boy insisted on playing Mommy!

Doctor: Miss Rivers, if you don't mind I'd like to go back to playing doctor with my next patient.

CHAPTER XIII

Is There a Father in the House?

Are daddies really necessary?

I say "yes." Just as every child needs a mother, it needs a daddy too. But what exactly is a daddy and who is he?

Daddy is the man who brings home the bacon—which these days costs a heck of a lot more than mother's milk.

Daddy is the thoughtful man who will suggest putting vodka in baby's bottle when he's crying.

Daddy is the guy who's quick to appear with the camera and just as quick to disappear when there's a diaper to be changed.

On the coldest of nights, he's the one who suddenly is only too happy to drive the babysitter home—once he notices that she's seventeen, nubile and has "welcome" written on her panties. That's who daddy is.

Still, while you're providing your child with his layette, furniture and toys, also try to provide a daddy. Remember: it's a wise child who knows its own father—before the blood tests are in . . .

Doctor: Let me assure you, fathers are needed by children of both sexes.

Joan: But they never seem to be around when mommy needs them.

Doctor: Unfortunately, after a hard day at the office daddy may not always feel up to the rigors of fatherhood. However, if he knows how important his company is to the child, he should be willing to devote a reasonable amount of time to him. Quality, rather than quantity, is what is important. One index to quality is the approving attitudes of the father. Fathers sometimes expect too much—especially of sons—and they get turned off if the youngster doesn't show immediate promise of genius or athletic prowess. This gives the child the sense of not adding up to very much.

Joan: But his psychiatrist's bills will add up to plenty.

Doctor: If the father is impatient or cranky, the little boy is apt to feel out

of tune with the whole world of male interests and draw closer to his mother and her interests.

Joan: Oh-oh! I'd hate to see a five-year-old boy doing bust development exercises.

Doctor: Of course, little girls need a loving daddy too.

Joan: Yes, but after 17 preferably not their own.

Doctor: A father, in appreciating and loving his little daughter, will give her confidence in herself and pleasure in being a girl.

Joan: But who wants to be a little girl these days? Everyone wants to be liberated—except me. I don't want to be liberated—I was never captured.

Doctor: Around the time children are three years old, they begin to think both their fathers and mothers are wonderful people.

Joan: A feeling destined to last ten gorgeous seconds.

Doctor: A father should share in disciplining the child. But too many fathers shy away from this job, particularly if they had fathers whose disciplining they resented. They don't want to be resented by their children, so they prefer to walk away from any unpleasantness.

Joan: Sure—let mommy do it. And let mommy get up at night. And let mommy change the dirty diapers. And let mommy clean up the messes and mend the clothes and wash the cuts and take out the splinters and what thanks does mommy get for all this? A hamburger on Mother's Day in McDonald's.

Doctor: Easy, easy, Miss Rivers. I agree with you. Fathers must help—even with the punishing. The child knows when he has punishment coming to him and when his father evades it he becomes all the more fearful. It's better for the father to clear the air. Not pleasant for the youngster, true, but he learns that he can survive it.

Joan: You know that old saying, "Spare the rod . . . we'll need it for hanging curtains."

Doctor: Just never forget—especially during punishing—you are a lot bigger than your child. So spank to *punish*—not to hurt. Also, the best place for a good wallop is the rear-end.

Joan: What happens if the father is never around? This would really upset a child. My friend Selma is a case in point. She had a tragic childhood. Her father died three years before she was born.

Doctor: There are a few things we should say about absent fathers.

Joan: The most printable of which is, "Where the hell is that bum?"

Doctor: Wherever he is, he should keep in touch.

Joan: Yes, and I guess it would be courteous to send him commencement and marriage announcements.

Doctor: He should not just be told the obvious things, like how much baby weighs or how tall he is or what his first words were, but also some of the tiny engaging details of baby's growth and development.

Joan: Such as, "Darling, wish you could be here this very moment to see little Johnny teething on your mother's fat thighs."

Doctor: Most importantly the father shouldn't be told that there are no problems whatsoever. That makes him feel irrelevant and not needed.

Joan: If he's gone too long, that's just what he'll be.

Doctor: On the other hand, you shouldn't burden him with decisions he can't handle from a distance or problems he can't do anything about.

Joan: Such as, "Guess what? I'm pregnant again."

Doctor: Now if the parents are divorced, what the mother should do is . . .

Joan: Make him pay a fortune in alimony.

Doctor: By all means, but if the father is not around, the child can still grow up without suffering any particular psychic damage. Much depends on the mother's spirit.

Joan: It would help if she actually had a large supply of spirits.

Doctor: As best she can, she should go on with her normal routine, keeping up with her outside interests and social activities. But remember, whatever the age or sex, the child needs to be friendly with other men if the father is gone. Grandfathers, cousins, scoutmasters, old family friends . . .

Joan: . . . *Young* family friends.

Doctor: All kinds of friendly men can give the child the male companionship he needs.

Joan: And even have some left over for mommy.

Doctor: If it's a boy, by the time he's two or so, he should be playing with other boys every day. Inviting lots of boys over to play at your house so your youngster can have lots of male companionship is a must.

Joan: Hey, I just thought of something. If there's no father around, the mother has to do all the disciplining . . . like getting the kid to bed on time.

Doctor: Of course, it's better when each parent can take his turn at it—but whoever does it should be cheerful but firm. Don't ask the child if he'd like to go to bed. Set a time and stick to it, but don't be so rigid that there can never be an exception. Like on Halloween or Christmas Eve . . .

Joan: . . . or the night Aunt Jane's will is going to be read.

Doctor: Preparing for bed should have a little ritual about it.

Joan: Little ritual! My God, you should see what I go through. First, off come the eyelashes, the eyeshadow, the eyeliner and my wiglet. Then off comes my Cross-My-Heart bra. Then out with the dentures. Then on with the creams and lotions and oils and salves. I'm so greasy, I get into bed and slide right out.

Doctor: The baby should have some hugs and kisses, be tucked in and read to a little bit, or maybe listen to a favorite record until he falls asleep. The stories shouldn't be scary or he's liable to have a nightmare.

Joan: Well, there goes every fairy tale I know—Hansel and Gretel getting shoved in the oven; Red Riding Hood chased by the wolf; and two of the three little pigs being eaten up. The only nice fairy story I know is the love of Batman for Robin.

Doctor: How much sleep a child needs varies. But you can't assume just because he's wide awake he's getting enough sleep. There may be any number of stimulating factors that are keeping him awake. As a rule of thumb, the average two and a half-year-old needs twelve hours of sleep at night and a nap of one to two hours during the day. This amount lessens gradually as he grows older.

Joan: I need a lot of sleep too. But I usually get it in little naps when I'm at the wheel on the freeway or when I'm making love.

Doctor: Another area of discipline is to get your child to perform certain tasks for himself. For example: a child starts to undress himself sometime between the ages of one and one and a half, and at about two has mastered the art. But getting his clothes on again is harder. However, let him try to do it himself and when you help him be diplomatic and don't help him too much. Again, the key word is patience. And when he does something right, be sure to praise him.

Joan: With all this talk about dressing and undressing, I've developed a chill. So may I ask you something, Doctor?

Doctor: Of course. What is it?

Joan: If we're through for today, do you mind if I put on my clothes?

DIAPER RASH GROWS ON YOU!

CHAPTER XIV

The First Three Years Are the Hardest—Until the Fourth

In the beginning there was my pregnancy, then delivery, and then diapers, formulas, colic, 2 a.m. feedings, temper tantrums, teething—and all the other joys too, too humorous to mention. But finally Melissa hit three and I saw a light at the end of the tunnel—Nursery School.

I was thrilled. At last I'd have time to myself. I thought nursery school would be good since it was really nothing more than an expensive stopgap between Sesame Street and bedtime.

It turned out that I was wrong as usual. I investigated and found out there were all kinds of nursery schools. One of the best known in my area was The Fanny Hill & Dale Country Day School. It was a bit too liberal for us. Not only did they have Washington and Lincoln's birthday off, they also took off on Margaret Sanger's. One mother who had pulled her Little Darling out told me they had taught arithmetic by using such problems as, "If Johnny has five marijuana cigarettes and smokes two, how many does he have left? How many does he *think* he has left?"

The next school we investigated was one in Hollywood—The Raquel Welch Nursery School. The name turned me off right away as I felt they would probably place too much emphasis on the plastic arts. Also, I didn't want Melissa to go to any "show biz" school. A friend of mine sent her child to one and it was terrible. When the kids auditioned for the school play, rumor had it that a "casting crib" was involved!

We finally settled on a nice simple one: The Jack and Jill Maximum Security Nursery School. Melissa spent many happy hours there painting, playing with blocks and working in clay.

Not only did she adore it, but she also adored her twenty-year-old teacher. She kept telling me how alike we were: the same eyes, the same hairdo, the same figure. To say the least, I was extremely flattered, but I think he was a bit miffed!

I remember telling my doctor about this . . .

Doctor: It's good that your child adores her teacher and that she is happy in school. School means rules and this is good. Lots of modern theories say that all a kid needs at home is love—no rules—and that children should be allowed to give full vent to their antisocial feelings. They say that if anything goes wrong, it has to be the parents' fault . . .

Joan: . . . except if it's an earthquake. Then it's Saint Andreas' fault.

Doctor: Many parents hate to discipline their children and therefore have a difficult time because they're guilt-ridden, and guilt gets in the way of handling a child easily. The child knows when he's way out of line and unconsciously wants to be stopped. If he consistently is not stopped, he will become a spoiled child. And nobody wants a spoiled child.

Joan: Because they smell bad?

Doctor: Problems often occur when parents had rough childhoods themselves. Perhaps they always had to be too "good" for their own good and now they get some kind of inner glee in seeing their own progeny act out all the aggressions they had to keep bottled up. Kidding themselves, of course, that they're being "modern" parents.

Joan: Remember Adam and Eve—and their delightful son, Cain! He really got away with murder.

Doctor: And he should have been stopped in childhood!

Joan: Everytime I did something bad, my mother would say, "How could you? After all the sacrifices I've made!" And she did make sacrifices for me. Once a week she would kill a chicken in front of my photograph.

Doctor: All the studies have shown that a child is happier if some standards of decently good behavior are met.

Joan: Of course he is. But mommy and daddy may have a dickens of a time meeting them.

Doctor: If he's being rude to his parents, he should be stopped. He'll get mad at you—but let him. And also let him know that his angry feelings are quite normal. Another tip to the wise parent is, "Tell them; don't ask them." You hear many a mother saying, "Shall we lunch now?" Or, "Shall we go sit on the potty now?" This is wrong.

Joan: Of course it is. Every kid knows there isn't such a thing as a potty built for two.

Doctor: Don't give him choices. Just lead him toward the appropriate activity. For instance, if your two-year-old is pushing a toy truck around the room and you sense he should be going to the bathroom, you might say, "Now let's drive the truck on a nice long trip to the bathroom." And don't get into the habit of giving him reasons why things should be done. Most of the reasons tend to have an "or else" kind of warning. "Don't poke Fluffy in the eye or his eye will fall out and he won't be able to see anything." You're warning him of unhappy consequences that can fill his young head with morbid thoughts.

Joan: When otherwise it could be filling up with sordid thoughts.

Doctor: If the youngster is in danger or endangering something or somebody else, remove him. It's not necessary to give explanations for everything. At a certain age, you can get into a real hassle trying to answer the interminable "Why?" "Shall we go out and take a walk now?" "Why?" "Because we need our exercise." "Why?" "Because it will help us grow strong." "Why?" And on into the night. So use your judgment and answer some whys but not all.

Joan: Why?

Doctor: The very small child knows he's new to the world and there's a lot he doesn't know. He depends on you to be his experienced guide.

Joan: The little fool!

Doctor: When his impulses are frustrated he may take it out on the floor or himself, pounding with hands and feet and yelling his head off, but don't be alarmed. A temper tantrum once in a while doesn't mean too much. If you see it coming, the best thing is to head it off with some pleasant distraction.

Joan: But you can't just start nursing him any old time and place. I know. I'll give him a rattle—with the snake still on the end of it.

Doctor: When the storm does break, keep out of the baby's way and take it easy until the thing subsides. There's no sense to a tantrum if there's no audience.

Joan: Good, I'll go on that long-deferred trip to Bermuda.

Doctor: Whatever you do, don't give in to his demand or he'll be throwing a tantrum every time there's a tug of wills.

Joan: Could it be a time to give him something to really yammer about? Like a belt in the butt?

Doctor: No, when a child is in the middle of a tantrum, it's no time to be angry with him or try to reason with him. The best thing is to try to find him some face-saving out. You can quietly disappear and hope the storm will soon blow over. Or if the baby's headstrong and he seems hell-bent on yelling you into an institution, after a while you might pop in with some friendly make-up overture. A hug and kiss and maybe a fun suggestion for something to do.

Joan: Such as, "Come on, Dickie, let's see who can hold his head longer under the bath water."

Doctor: Where your mettle will really be tested is when the baby throws a temper tantrum in some very public place. If you can manage it, pick him up with a cheery expression and hurry into some quiet corner where your passions can cool.

Joan: Such as my car. That way the kid can scream all he wants to and get away with murder, and I can laugh all I want to and get away with thirty-two bucks worth of free groceries.

Doctor: And don't be thrown by the breath holding bit.

Joan: Thrown! I'm delighted when a kid holds his breath—especially if he's just eaten garlic or smoked a cigar.

Doctor: When a child holds his breath during a tantrum, ignore it and keep your cool. Remember, he will stop holding his breath.

Joan: The moment he loses consciousness.

Doctor: Talking about tempers brings us to the subject of punishment. To punish or not to punish.

Joan: Is *not* the question when a kid deserves it.

Doctor: Yes, it is. Some parents' discipline seems to be firm enough to hold up without resorting to punishment.

Joan: I've always felt it isn't hard to rear a child as long as it has a rear.

Doctor: The thing to remember is that punishment is never the vital element in training a child. It's being loved and learning to love back. When a child starts to think his parents are wonderful and he wants to imitate them, he does a lot to civilize himself. But he needs direction. In football parlance, he's the player but you're the coach.

Joan: I hate to think of my kid growing up to be a football player. They're so dumb. I was with one in an elevator once. The operator called out the floors and he tackled her.

Doctor: Day by day, it's the job of the parent to keep the child in training with love and strength and a reasonable show of predictability. If the system breaks down and too many rules get broken, the time may be at hand for severer measures.

Joan: Then it's twenty laps around the track and no wine, women or song for a week.

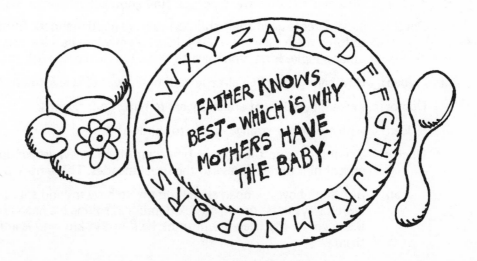

Doctor: There's been a reaction in recent times against spanking. But if it's a choice of spanking or prolonged nagging or trying to make a child feel unduly guilty, I'll take the spanking.

Joan: Easy for you to say. Who'd dare to spank a doctor?

Doctor: Some authorities recommend that if you're going to spank, never do it in anger. Of course, sometimes the go-to-your-room ploy works. But the danger there is the child might begin to think of his room as a prison.

Joan: I'd have to do a lot of redecorating to make it look that good.

Doctor: Other parents delegate the naughty child to sit off by himself in a special chair, but the thing I don't like at all is threats, especially the kind that are totally ridiculous and can't be followed through on. For example: "If you don't go to sleep this instant, the big bad wolf is going to come and get you." Also, parents who always have to resort to punishment obviously have a problem, and the problem is themselves. In some way they are inviting bad behavior from their children and then they act surprised when it comes. These people need help.

Joan: Who doesn't! But where do you find good help these days?

Doctor: Most parents want their children to have good manners, but it's hard to force them on a child. He'll learn them when he's learned to like other people. First, you have to make him feel easy with strangers.

Joan: How can I when I've already told him never to speak to one?

Doctor: I mean, people that are strangers to him. Your friends.

Joan: Who are pretty strange, come to think of it.

Doctor: The thing is don't introduce him right off to a new grown-up and expect him to respond with the usual niceties. This embarrasses him.

Joan: But think how it embarrasses mommy to have my kid stand there with his eyes cast down, struck dumb and rolling his head around like a yo-yo. My friends will think he's a fresh kid who is imitating them.

Doctor: For approximately the first three years, a child needs time to size up a stranger. While he does this, it's best to steer the conversation away from him, rather than making him the subject under discussion. When he sees you talking casually to a new person for a few minutes, he might feel comfortable enough to break into the conversation.

Joan: With some choice announcement like, "Mommy, Spot's in heat again."

Doctor: Admittedly his conversational gambits might not be for high society. But if a child's feeling of friendliness toward others keeps growing, it'll be reflected in more acceptable conversation.

Joan: Which means all he'll ever discuss is having sex and tax shelters . . . or is it having sex in tax shelters?

Doctor: The best way for a child to learn to be kind and polite is to watch his own family.

SEYMOUR XAVIER SCHAINHOLZ, M.D.

Dear Miss Rivers:

It was a pleasure to finally get through to you on the phone the other day and I could hardly believe that it was Melissa who answered it.

At your suggestion I am resubmitting my statement. I can well appreciate your confession that you threw out the last one thinking it was "junk mail."

Naturally I hope I have better luck this time around.

Most sincerely,

Joan: In that case, my kid may have to look for foster parents. My husband is so rude to me! The other day I said to him, "Nothing I do pleases you anymore. I'm going home to Mother." He said, "*That* pleases me."

Doctor: A child does have to learn to say "please" and "thank you" and "I'm sorry" when dealing with people. But teach your baby gently. And do it in private to save him embarrassment.

Joan: You mean wait until you get home before you tell Johnny he shouldn't have asked nice Mrs. Johnson next door why she has a moustache?

Doctor: Yes. Unless Mrs. Johnson happens to be proud of her moustache and purposely cultivated it.

Joan: To go with her mink coat, no doubt.

Doctor: You'll find between the ages of two and three, the child goes through a balky, contrary phase. He thinks he is being bossed too much, but is bossy himself. He wants to do everything his own way. He can't make up his mind and once he does, he immediately wants to change it. But cheer up. There are better days coming.

Joan: If you believe in the hereafter.

Doctor: To a degree let him have his head. Allow a little more time for getting things done. Let him do as much as he can for himself. Steer him gently toward the "must-do" things with a pleasant flow of chatter. Sometimes you see a dawdling child with a mother who prods him from morning to night.

Joan: Now let me join in with the refrain: "He wasn't born that way. It's his mother's doing."

Doctor: You've guessed the villain. The mother. That nervous, nagging mother who's always anticipating that he won't do what he should. All this pressure on the child naturally sets up the balkiness that makes the prodding seem necessary. The wise thing is to give him a reasonable chance to do what he should be doing. If that doesn't work, remind him gently to shape up, but remember small children love to do things that get them dirty, like mucking around in the dirt and smearing themselves with mud. It makes them feel good.

Joan: Just as it makes mommy feel good. I once spent $25 for a full mud pack and I never looked better. Then about the third day, the mud fell off.

Doctor: It's unhealthy to limit such activities for they are natural and necessary. If he's thwarted, it'll make him hold back in other ways and he may not grow into the warm, spontaneous life-embracing little person you hope he's going to be.

Joan: When does that warm, spontaneous, life-embracing little person get out from underfoot and start making it on his own?

Doctor: Three is none too early to start your youngster in school if he is in an area without other children. In fact it's highly desirable. Some mothers say, "Oh, I think I'll wait another year. Little Janie will get so much more out of it when she's four." This misses the point of nursery school. The value is not so much in what they get out of classes or activities, but in the children's joy in one another's companionship.

Joan: And there's the joy mommy gets in sharing her little treasure with others, since the sharing takes place away from her. On days off from school, I find that sandboxes are great substitutes for baby sitters. I know of several dumb kids who just sit in them for hours waiting for the tide to come in.

Doctor: Whether it's playing in a sand box or backyard mud, just don't make your child feel he is doing something really messy or disgusting.

Joan: Like engaging in sex play?

Doctor: You'll have to contend with that too at about this time.

Joan: I'd love to contend with it if I didn't already have the kid to contend with.

Doctor: We know that interest in sex begins practically at birth. But even so, parents find it upsetting to see young children engaged in sex play with themselves or others.

Joan: Can you wonder? You want the best for your kids and all that. But who wants to see a three-year-old already making out better than you are?

Doctor: Around the age of three, there's natural curiosity about why little boys are made differently from little girls. Unless this curiosity is satisfied, youngsters may go on harboring fears about themselves. Little David sees that his baby sister doesn't have a penis and he wonders if something happened to it. Then you explain that there are two kinds of people. He's like his father and Uncle Harry and Cousin Joe, and his baby sister is like Mommy and Grandma and Aunt Helen.

Joan: And Uncle Charlie—after his trip to Denmark. Charlie had a change-of-sex operation and now I'm so confused as to what he is, that for his birthday I gave him a set of his and hers towels.

Doctor: Little girls need to be cheerfully assured, too, that nothing has happened to them—that they never had a penis and it's just fine to be the way they are.

Joan: It must be. Look who gets all the obscene phone calls.

Doctor: Also, remember that the handling of the genitals begins very early. Around the age of three it may be related to the fears we were just discussing. This is a time when children's feelings are very intense. In any event, you discourage it—as you do sex play between youngsters —but don't act shocked or outraged or disgusted.

Joan: The way I did on my wedding night?

Doctor: With or without your help a child's sex education keeps expanding. But he'll be better off if he can go to you with his questions.

Joan: That way, he'll be kept in the dark that much longer.

Doctor: The conscientious mother can sometimes go into more detail with explanations than the child wants or can absorb. A three-year-old will probably be asking where babies come from. The best answer to that is: "From a seed that grows inside mommy." Period. One thing I'd advise against is blaming babies on the stork.

Joan: And how! I never heard of anyone making out with a stork! I'll just tell him what my mother told me. The recipe for having a baby is simply to take one man and one woman and mix well.

Doctor: Much of this education will come gradually through contact with their peers. In kindergarten, they will probably get the chance to take care of pets. This is extremely educational.

Joan: Especially monkeys. To this day I run to the zoo every Sunday to watch. A friend of mine used to squint and pretend it was a guy and a girl doing it in fur coats.

Doctor: Children of three, as we've said, have a pretty clear idea of their sex identities. It's really a wonderful time in the parents' lives. The children idolize them. Boys want to be like their fathers and girls want to be like their mothers. Little boys and girls develop romantic feelings about the parents of the opposite sex. Young David is likely to say to his mother, "Mommy, I want to marry you."

Joan: Mommy could do a lot worse—and probably already has.

Doctor: The wise parent thanks his child for the compliment but tactfully explains that he already is married, and that the child will grow up and pick out his own wife.

Joan: You know what, Doc?

Doctor: What?

Joan: After our many little talks, I've come to the conclusion that in spite of all the work and mess and bother involved, there's nothing like having a child. Why, I'd rather have my darling baby than a million dollars.

Doctor: Really?

Joan: Absolutely! Because when you have a million dollars, you want another million, but when you have a kid . . .

CHAPTER XV

You'll Still Be Seeing Your Gynecologist . . .
and He'll Be Seeing Everything

Okay, you've had your baby. The kid is doing fine and you're a fulfilled woman at last. So what do you do now?

As a mature, informed woman you know you should go to the gynecologist for check-ups every six months, right? But no woman likes to go to the gynecologist. And without the shield of your tummy in front of you, you suddenly feel *very* aware of the situation and how much you dread these embarrassing visits.

First of all, he never gets to see the pretty underwear that you put on just for him—thanks to his nasty nurse, who is obviously in love with him and understandably resents your superior looks. She's not going to let you flaunt any seductive dainties before his eyes. So she puts you in that little room and makes you take off everything. And I mean *everything*. (I had one nurse once who made me take off a corn plaster.) Then she puts you in that little white paper dress with the slit up the back and hands you a huge bottle.

"Here," she says haughtily. "The doctor will want a sample of your urine."

This always hurts me. After all these years, either he wants it or he doesn't. I'm tired of giving free samples!

After the sample bit is over, the nurse puts you on that table with the paper covering and puts your feet in the stirrups. "Move down, move down," she keeps saying. I don't know about you, but I *can't* move. I'm stuck to the paper. Then she covers you up with that sheet that covers up nothing and tells you to relax. "Doctor will be right in."

There you are alone . . . for eternities. Facing you *revoltingly* is that cabinet filled with those shiny, enormous instruments that could not possibly fit inside a mother of fourteen, much less little me.

Finally . . . the good doctor makes his entrance. He takes one glance at your immaculate body which is fresh out of a three-hour tub bath *and* he has the nerve and tactlessness to don a pair of rubber gloves!

Somehow, I always find myself in the hands of doctors who think they are comedians. I want to say to them, "You stick to your scalpeling and leave the jokes to me." Because I don't think doctors should be funny. What ails us is not a laughing matter.

I had a friend, if I may digress a moment, who underwent major surgery. When he came out of his anesthetic, the doctor was by his bed chuckling to himself.

"Mr. X," said the doctor (a shortened version of my friend's original name, which was Xsky), "I have both good news and bad news for you."

"Give me the bad news first," whispered Mr. X.

"Well, we had to remove both your legs."

"What's the good news?"

"We sold your slippers," said the doctor, cracking up.

In a gynecologist, the last thing you're looking for is fun and games. You're distraught and humiliated enough at the absurd position you're in without having the doctor, while he's examining you, go, "Coochie coochie coo."

Part II in the gynecological exam is equally off-putting. You sit with the doctor in his modern, plant-filled office and the conversation takes such an indelicate turn. It may be just my repressed upbringing but somehow I hardly think "discharges" is a fit subject to be discussing with a mature, attractive man, unless you're talking about the mustering out of military personnel.

What also gets me crazy is having to fill the prescription the doctor gives you. The cost of the pills he prescribes is exorbitant. I get around this monthly drain by taking a pill every *other* day. My gynecologist found out about this and said I was playing a dangerous game—"Baby Roulette."

So what's the solution? We have to go to the gynecologist every six months and be examined. My best advice is to find a good one and to keep the relationship on a strictly professional basis. In other words, someone outside your social circle and whom you're unlikely to meet in a social situation.

I'll never forget the time I went to a dinner party and drew for my dinner partner my very own gynecologist. "Hello, Joan," he smiled. As I had all my clothes on and my face was almost totally camouflaged under my heavy evening makeup, I couldn't understand how he recognized me. "Hey, Doc," I blurted out, "how'd you know it was me?" "Easy," said my doctor, grinning, "when you dropped your fork."

SEYMOUR XAVIER SCHAINHOLZ, M.D.

Miss Rivers:

I was most upset when the check you claimed was "in the mail" never arrived.

Your prompt payment of my bill would be so much appreciated, needless to say, at this particular time.

Sincerely,

Closing Monologue

Hello, Doctor, I'm sorry to disturb you on a Tuesday as I know this is your morning to make out your inflated Blue Shield reports, but I just had to talk to you . . . Yes, I'll be brief . . . You see, my darling baby is three now and off to nursery school and so smart that when my husband and I discuss anything in front of her, we have to purposely misspell words. Plus the child is gorgeous. She has my eyes, my nose, my mouth, my hair. The only thing that worries me a bit is one day I might need them back. . . . I *am* getting to the point, Doc . . . You see, I have never looked or felt better, if I do say so myself. But I don't have to. Why only the other day, our garage mechanic said, "That's some chassis you've got there," and he wasn't looking at my car. The stretch marks are practically all gone and with lots of workouts at my gym I've got my old figure back, or what's even better, I haven't got my old figure back, but a new and firmer one. And I've bought me a new wardrobe of six divine slack suits so I won't have to shave my legs all winter and next month my darling daughter and I will sit for our portrait. We have such a close relationship. We're almost like mother and daughter . . . Wait, Doc, hold on . . . just two minutes more . . . My husband has never adored me more than now that I've fulfilled my role as M*O*T*H*E*R. Why, he's put me on a pedestal and, even though I have to dust it, it's worth it. But you see, finally, after four difficult years, I have the time to dust if I want to and decorate my home and go out to mad lunches with girl friends. Stop rushing me, Doc, I am getting to the point and just remember, I knew you before abortions were legalized. In those days, you were glad to get a call . . . Anyhow, now that I'm a Ma, I've decided to go back to school and get my M.A. I was a philosophy major in college. What good did philosophy do me these last couple of years with a screaming, wet kid on my hands? All I could use it for was to prove to myself that the dirty diapers didn't really exist. Oh, and the joy of joys, I'm back to reading again.

Serious reading, I mean. Not Spock. Spillane . . . Okay, okay, I know you're not interested in all this garbage . . . So, why am I calling you if everything is so terrific? Well, you see, Doc, up until this morning I really was the happiest and fittest of women. But I woke up feeling perfectly horrible. Headache. Heartburn. Nausea. I felt absolutely bushed. And I blush to bring up such intimate symptoms, especially as I know your service is listening in, but my you-know-what is long, long overdue and . . .

HIGH CLASS COLLECTION AGENCY

Dear Ms. Robers,

Our client, Seemore X. Shainholz, gave us his bill for collection.

It would be a pity if a nice goil like you were to come out of a club one night and find herself in the presence of our enforcers. They are not a good audience. Pay up or we will repossess.

Hy Klass

SECOND LETTER FROM A REAL DOCTOR—

Dearest ~~Daughter, Joanie, Jean~~, Ms. Rivers,

I have in front of me your request for approval of your manuscript, <u>Having a Baby Can Be a Scream</u>. First of all, let me state that signing the request, "Your adoring daughter, Joan," is the kind of begging behavior which your mother and I tried to break you of many years ago. Your dog learned to have a sense of dignity. I don't know why you didn't.

Putting aside your special pleading and dealing with the manuscript itself, I can only say that conveying sound medical and psychological advice in terms comprehensible to the average person is strictly against all known and approved medical procedures, and I certainly cannot be a party to it. Next thing you know, they will be asking us to write our prescriptions legibly.

Anyhow, getting back to your manuscript, all the advice you have in there is very sound and correct. Lord knows, it is what your mother and I used in raising you. On second thought, maybe it is not such good advice.

Nothing else is new, except the pond's frozen over, but in spite of this we had a bumper crop of rutabagas this year, which surprised everyone as we live in the heart of New York City.

Please keep in touch--but not too closely. A large check in the mail each month is the best way as it serves to tell us that your memory is functioning and that you are doing well.

                     Your loving father,

                           Meyer L. Rivers M.D.

                           Meyer L. Rivers, M.D.

P.S. Mother thought that this might be a good opportunity to tell you that you're not ours. We were originally going to write you a separate letter--but why waste postage?